T0348931

A
Living

**Also by Michael D. Stein**

Probabilities

The White Life

The Lynching Tree

In the Age of Love

This Room Is Yours

The Rape of the Muse

The Lonely Patient: How We Experience Illness

The Addict: One Patient, One Doctor, One Year

Pained: Uncomfortable Conversations about the Public's Health

Broke: Patients Talk about Money with Their Doctor

Me vs. Us: A Health Divided

Accidental Kindness: A Doctor's Notes on Empathy

The Picture of Health

The Turning Point: Reflections on a Pandemic

# A Living

## WORKING-CLASS AMERICANS TALK TO THEIR DOCTOR

MICHAEL D. STEIN, M.D.

MELVILLE HOUSE
BROOKLYN / LONDON

A LIVING

First published in 2025 by Melville House

First Melville House Printing: January 2025

Melville House Publishing
46 John Street
Brooklyn, NY 11201
and
Melville House UK
Suite 2000
16/18 Woodford Road
London E7 0HA

mhpbooks.com
@melvillehouse

ISBN: 978-1-68589-190-9
ISBN: 978-1-68589-189-3 (eBook)

Library of Congress Control Number: 2024948503

Designed by Beste M. Doğan

Printed in the United States of America

1 3 5 7 9 10 8 6 4 2

A catalog record for this book is available from the Library of Congress

*To dearest Martha and Tom,*
*Makers of pies and buildings*

The intelligence of the waitress in motion,
the reflective welder, the strategy of the guy on the
assembly line. This is something I've
learned: the thought it takes to do physical work.
—MIKE ROSE, *The Mind At Work*

# CONTENTS

## TO THE READER

This book contains the stories of real people. They share their lives in confidence, and I must honor that trust. I have changed names, some physical descriptions, and medical concerns of the speakers to protect anonymity. Anyone recognizable is coincidental.

# INTRODUCTION

Because I am a primary care doctor in a mid-sized industrial city in the northeastern United States where small manufacturing still exists (although the unions and the mills and factories where my patients' parents worked have mostly disappeared), I often see people who work with their hands. My patients are the frontline workers who remain hidden from top-income Americans; they live in neighborhoods I don't know. Few of my patients are in the nation's highest income strata. In 2019, the year before COVID-19 arrived, 62 percent of people in the top quarter of American income were able to work remotely, as opposed to 9 percent of the bottom quarter. Based on this simple statistic, anyone could have predicted that an airborne infectious agent would affect these essential occupations disproportionately.

In 2020, the first year of COVID-19, deaths differed by occupation in the United States. The highest death rates were seen, by risk order, in construction workers, transportation workers (public transit, trucks), retail workers (grocery, convenience, drugstore), correctional officers, home health aides, nurses, cooks, factory workers, and material movers (bulldozer operators). In the news reports and statistics, people filling these jobs requiring physical labor were called "frontline workers" or "essential workers." Essential work was typically low-wage labor that was taken for granted, mostly invisible to those who could work remotely from home. People of color were more likely than other workers to be in essential jobs. During COVID-19, essential meant "obligatory" for those who took the daily risk of getting sick in order to support themselves and their families. They worked paycheck to paycheck, meal to meal. COVID-19 shone a spotlight on the special risk to the well-being of certain workers. But as that attention fades, we are likely to forget the demanding physical labor of these individuals even as the national retirement age creeps past sixty-five and our national policies ask them to work longer, continuing the toll on their bodies.

Two-thirds of Americans do jobs that require physical labor. During the worst of the COVID-19 outbreak, it became clear that many jobs could potentially kill you. Following the pandemic years and the death-by-occupation data I learned, I found myself asking my patients more than I thought I ever would about their work, which so notably drives physical and mental health, and more clearly than ever before—even in non-pandemic times—delineates identity and complicates our notions of equality and fairness.

Are you working now?

Why not?

Do you ever go to work sick?

What part of work do you like the most? Hate the most?

What did you want to be when you were sixteen?

Do you imagine retiring?

Do you think you will ever be able to retire?

For all of us, our job is what we know best. But its peculiarities are unknown to others. My patients talk to me about jobs I am familiar with and jobs I didn't know existed. The conversations I've written down here come after a pandemic that killed over one million Americans, some of them my former patients.

I spend my life as a doctor at work in this circular suite of offices, among a small group of medical colleagues, shuttling between nearly identical examining-tabled rooms, going round and round like a bobbing piece of wood in the eddies of my day. But it doesn't feel repetitive like the factory work I hear about. Each patient feels like the first and only one. Every day I must get things right when I diagnose and treat, and I hope I get very few very wrong. It is a high bar—the challenge must remain a fixation for me to do this work well. My patients take time off from work (unpaid) to see me, so I always take them seriously.

My patients are not hard for me to like; they display their best behaviors with me. I've always admired people who are good at things I am not—mechanics who understand engines, people who know how to build a house. I like to be able to tell my patients who barely finished high school that they are experts at things I have no aptitude for, that they can see things that I can't, that their work is a richly layered skill. This makes them smile even if they're thinking: *This doctor here still makes more money than I do, the lucky bastard.* But they know I'm right. As a patient once said to me, "Guys with high school degrees fix things. Guys with college degrees screw things up." To which I answered, "You better hope that's not the case here."

**MANY OF MY PATIENTS COME** to my office directly from work. They wear stiff, steel-toed boots, donut shop uniforms with first name pins, florescent-green road-crew vests, waiters' black pants with a sheen, heavy flannel shirts, canvas overalls, company insignia on white polos, knee pads. They wear dust and paint drips, tomato sauce and soot, oil stains and plaster nibs; they smell of coffee and sweat, overheated machines and cigarettes. During an exam, my nose is close to their scalps. With each visit, I rediscover the pungency of direct patient care in this place that between visits smells sweetly of spray disinfectant and leftover brownies. My exam room is clean and orderly until they put their helmets and belts and knapsacks and keychains down on the chairs. I have seen these patients of mine hurt and bloodied from work in factories, nursing homes, boat yards, and warehouses, on trucks and train tracks. Sometimes, their work leaves fingers broken, knees swollen, wrists burnt, shoulders dislocated, forearms numb—or it takes away years. But I've also seen my patients hurt by *not* working—this is its own affliction with a particular emotional toll. Work can heal them too.

**I HAVE LEARNED THAT THERE** can be no meaningful discourse about health divorced from where people work, how many hours, which shift, the nature of the work, the amount of money they make.

This book is not about the sociology of occupational hazard. There are certainly harsh conditions in some industries, and many of my patients are exposed to extreme physical risks. I do not offer a comprehensive list of work-related morbidity or of jobs—because of where I live, I do not have miners or hog farmers or active-duty soldiers in my practice. Nor am I writing about ethically troubling work; here, "getting your hands dirty" is meant literally. I can't include every type of job or represent all workers in the United States; for instance, I leave out parents who do physical work looking after their children, which is an essential job too, even if unwaged. Likewise, not all the people featured here are poor. Some are trapped in what they do because they have no better-paying options. As one of my patients said, "I am not happy to be there. Happy to have a job, yes. But I don't come bopping into work in the morning, brimming with joy. That's just not my job." Others like their jobs. Work can be a ritual, or it can be urgent. I am not writing about hourly wages or advancement, about the quality of work or the inequality of workers, although I include as interruptions to my patients' words some peculiarly American policies that affect workers, and I am as aware as any taxpayer that investment in our economy has discounted the making of stuff.

Instead, *A Living* introduces you to the lives and concerns of people who work with their hands, who do manual labor, whose work not long ago was deemed essential, a category that has been almost forgotten now five years after the peak of COVID-19. As this large and various collection of workers ages, many of their health problems are work-related, though of course not all, what with lupus and gallstones and other conditions that come simply from bad luck. When it was established in 1935, Social Security was intended to sustain people once they could no longer physically work. Just as COVID-19 affected workers differentially, raising the retirement age needs to be thought about differentially as well, because it's not going to affect every occupation the same. COVID-19 has helped us to ask: What do people deserve?

This book is about what my patients say *about* work when they speak to me about the activities *at* work, but also their imaginings and yearnings, and what's lost, besides a paycheck, when work disappears. Listening to patients speak about work is, for me, a way of looking for the emotional narrative, the psychological explanation, the personal history, which, by nature, always interest me, but these can also explain how the body breaks, and caring for the broken mind and body is my job, my daily work, where I go for meaning, belonging, and continuity.

In the United States, about half of the labor force is employed in working-class jobs, defined as manual labor, service industry, and clerical work. Fewer than 2 percent of members of Congress worked in such jobs before being elected.

# A
# Living

# 1

# IDENTITY

I absorbed my ideas about work growing up in a family of social workers and schoolteachers. I've believed, for all my life, that work is good. Mostly this belief reflects the fact that I've always liked to work. I liked cutting grass and shoveling snow and delivering papers as a boy—I certainly would have liked them less if I wasn't paid—and later working in a restaurant kitchen. My doctoring now is a lot of paper and computer work, with talk and examination time built in. I am an employee—I get reviewed; I can get fired. But it is a job that is satisfying, a source of pleasure and accomplishment and status and money. And most of all, identity. Most days I say, "I *am* a doctor," rather than, "I *work* as a doctor." On my best days, I make other people feel better and taken care of. In a good work life, you are also trying to make yourself happy.

Whether or not a certain line of work is shameful or honorable is culturally relative. One of the oldest prejudices, at least among the upper classes in many societies, has been against physical work. Plato thought bodily labor was degrading, that people's souls "are bowed and mutilated by their vulgar occupations." Drudgery, repetitive work, made people unfit for citizenship, Aristotle suggested, which seems odd given that before he was a teacher he worked as a mason. The disparagement of manual labor was not only Western. In

Confucian China, educated gentlemen grew their fingernails long to signal they did not work with their hands. For two thousand years, from the Romans to the mid-nineteenth century, the idea of having a job was an abomination: you were placing yourself in a position of subordination. Work was a fundamental attack on human dignity and human rights, and no person with any integrity or self-respect should submit themselves to it. Still, apprenticeship and the guild work of crafts and trades created traditions for the "hand-made," as well as systems of solidarity.

Factories, when they were established, required the coordinated labor of hundreds of people paid by the hour, and the result was that leisure became sharply delineated from work. Workers were offered a deal: do whatever you like with your time off so long as it doesn't damage your usefulness on the job. A hierarchy was established: work was seen as the real point of existence; leisure was merely an opportunity for recovery and replenishment (make sure you don't have a hangover because it affects your work), for the purpose of further work. Industrial work wasn't sufficiently meaningful to be the point of existence—you did it for the money, not for its intrinsic satisfactions. Its value was what it could get you when you weren't working.

In more recent centuries certain religious and utopian communities such as the Shakers, the Transcendentalists, and the Amish explicitly affirmed manual labor's value as part of an egalitarian outlook. The thinker and the worker could be the same person. As a binary setup, the idea of above- and below-the-neck learning has always made me uncomfortable. Intellectual processes are rarely stripped out of physical work, I've found when speaking to patients. Knowledge is necessary to be good at anything. Welding, bricklaying, hair-cutting, or construction requires that one troubleshoots, solves problems, makes decisions on the fly. Working with your hands is a kind of thinking. What's going well? What's not, and how can you fix it? With most work, you need a blend of formal training with hands-on experience. Those who blend best do the best work.

# CLAMMING: DENNIS

"You have a rake at the end of a pipe. You can get thirty to a hundred and shake them out of the rake. Put them in a bucket. Throw some back.

"There were days I'd come in with five thousand clams and get twenty or twenty-two cents apiece. I could pay my bills."

He has sun-ripened hands and short, prematurely gray hair. His skinny legs don't match his wide rakeman's chest. He has returned to see me because his sleep is bad, but I know his problems are deeper because he is talking about clamming in the past tense.

"So does that mean you're not going out anymore?" I ask.

"Every day was an adventure on the water. I felt strong. Not a lot of people did what I did. I felt special. I came home and I was tired. I ate, slept, and did it again."

Work has always been his life's constant. The late-afternoon light comes in through the big, unopenable, dusty window of my office in gray and filtered lines. He doesn't look satisfied with himself. He loved clamming more than anything; he wouldn't deny it. Which perhaps is his only hope to stop drinking and get back to work.

"I do still have my own boat," he says, as if he just remembered. He's changed to the present tense. "It's about self-discipline. You're not paid if you don't go."

How long had it been since he was on the water?

I have known him for eight years and have always been attracted to the hardness of his life, its lack of sentimentality, but also his search for romance and love.

# BUS: LON

"By the end of the day, I got this whole-body vibration. It feels like my bones are disintegrating, my back is shaken up so much. Some of them step on and are perfectly nice and smile; I'm picking up nurses and nannies and maids in the morning. And there's others who are having a bad day and get on saying things to me they shouldn't say, racial stuff, like they have the right to mistreat me because I'm driving them around. I've had a handful of quarters thrown at me. I've been spit at. But I make a very decent living, get really good health insurance, and a pension after twenty-five years of service."

He wears a back brace, Velcro-strapped, which holds his upper body stiff and keeps his breaths shallow like he's been deflated.

Can you be unhappy and not know it? At the end of most days, I wouldn't be able to tell you if I was happy or unhappy. The doctor must *act* happy. It is what patients who are down, who are no longer getting dressed for work, expect.

# THE WEEK: JEFF

"I get home at 6:00 PM. By the time I take a shower and eat and make my lunch for the next day, it's 7:30, and I go to bed at 8:00 because I wake up at 4:30 AM to be at work at 5:45. Sometimes I sleep until 4:35 to get that extra five minutes. I do literally nothing but work. I'm exhausted by Saturday, but that's when my granddaughters come over. They change my outlook, perk me up—but exhaust me more."

I can see him resisting the temptation for melancholy.

"Sunday, I catch up. I'm tired. I used to play golf or softball or go to the bar; now I don't leave the house. A heating pad and Advil are my best friends."

# TITRATION: CHRIS

"My anxiety goes down without alcohol, and when I work a lot, I don't drink. When I work a little, I drink. But when I don't work at all, I also don't drink because I don't have any panic attacks."

I can see he is trying to figure out the full equation of himself. There is a matter-of-fact set to his mouth. He is not at home in the world.

"Maybe I need a different line of work where I'm not having people depend on me like they do when I'm their waiter."

## HANDS-ON: POLLY

"Around the holidays, everyone wants their pet groomed. I love bathing the dogs. When you're done, and if they let you blow-dry them, they're soft and clean. Their attitude is different. As though they're smiling."

Her loud voice always surprises me when I'm expecting low and calming.

"Dogs want to eat me when I do their nails. We have to use a muzzle if they growl, and get someone to hold them; they don't like me and remember me the next time: they approach me slowly. They're sad afterward. One dog has hated me his whole life and hides when he sees me.

"The worst part is the anal glands on either side of their bum. You squeeze out nasty stuff. I get $15 for that, but it's not glamorous. It's a putrid smell that never goes away. I've had it squirt onto my face and hair. It's sort of funny afterward but disgusting when it happens."

She smiles. She has knobby fingers and flat palms.

"I wanted to be a vet. I wanted to work with animals, but I figured out how much schooling was, and I didn't want to be in classes for six years with all those books—that was too much. I went to school for grooming instead when I was nineteen, eight weeks only. Now I own one book, a few tools—clippers, mat splitters, brushes, combs—and it's all hands-on."

## POWER STRUCTURE: EDWIN

"I loved selling drugs.

"I think it was the power. The power of knowing people were at your mercy."

He is older now, and that life is behind him, and he is trying to be honest with himself.

"I always used girls as my sellers. You can't trust guys. They want to push you out, take your place.

"I had a false sense of popularity. I knew everyone downtown, walking around all night.

"I got arrested a few times. I never took it personally. The cops do their job; I do mine."

## FREE: BEN

"I've had a lot of jobs, but I'd cut hair for free. That didn't feel like going to work. It was creative, creating something from nothing. That feeling lasts with you. You got to learn something, fix it in your brain, transfer it to your hands, and make it come out of your fingers.

"The first time I picked up scissors, I wasn't bad. Three weeks into school, and my teacher offered me a job in his salon."

# BOAT-BUILDING: TIM

"There are about thirty pieces to a thirty-two-foot boat—the pan, the wells. I take the chopper gun, this fiberglass and resin mix, and shoot it into the boat mold. I pop the mold from the shape with this gel coat plug. I put on the first layer of chop and then add different layers, tighter weaves, Cormat or balsa layers, rolls of material. I work the air out with a squeegee."

He has shoulder-length hair and recurrent right elbow tendinitis. He wears flip-flops year-round.

"I love the work, but I hate the dirt of it. My clothes get hard from the resin. My shoes' soles become uneven so I hobble around. I throw my shirt away at the end of the week. Or I can wear a Tyvek suit, but those zippers always break, and I have to throw it away. Every week I buy cheap new clothes at Savers or the Salvation Army. I smell bad. People ask me what the smell is. 'Pure chemical,' I say.

"I can't hear in the shop. The flange is cutting, and the grinding guy is taking excess trim off the mold, and the saws and the fans are running all the time.

"It's uncomfortable to wear a respirator mask, so I don't. But it's not healthy. People in the industry have lung issues at forty or fifty, but what am I going to do? I wanted to be a conservation officer, work outdoors. This is about as far from that as could be."

He treats himself to one line of cocaine once a week on Friday, his petty rebellion, his private pleasure.

# THEY COULDN'T: JEANETTE

"My last job had a fast pace all day. The money was good. The people were nice. The worst part was the drive to work, so I gave it up to walk five minutes down the street from my house to Dunkin.'

"But there were children working there. They couldn't pour coffee; they couldn't do it. All they had to do was pour and put the lid on, and they couldn't. They asked for help constantly. And they didn't show up. No one fired them. They continued to work."

Their laziness seems unreasonable to her.

"So I went back to the old place. I don't have to teach children; the staff there has common sense."

# WRESTLING: JARED

"It was my dream since I was a nine-year-old. My friend Jerry's mom recorded us wrestling in front of the TV where we were watching wrestling."

A boy's joy sneaks into his voice.

"I loved when they fell off the ropes or fell out of the ring. It's like you're putting on a story. You want the audience to believe—it has to be believable, even if they don't like it."

He exudes agreeableness, and it is hard to imagine him looking mean and serious, although I've seen his shoulders round and thicken up over the past months.

"When I joined up and started training, I understood that even if it's scripted it still takes a toll on the body. It hurts. The collar and elbow tie-up. You need to look like you're struggling for position. You get bruises on the inside of the biceps. You bruise up until your body is used to taking that kind of beating. There are different kinds of bumps.

"The script is: you start with who wins and work backwards. Pass the plan for the next move through the referee. I like the psychology behind it."

# ENDING: KIM

"I worked as a bartender for two years. But then, as with any job, I had had enough. You work late, you can't stand the smell of alcohol—although it also makes you want to drink—you can't take the drunk people, who really are very annoying."

At first, I sense she is downplaying the difficulty of those years. Then she returns to her usual optimism.

"I was good at remembering the details about people, even if I didn't remember their names, but that made me good with the regulars, so the money was good."

# MAKING: ANDRE

"I've been making N95 masks, third shift. That time fits with my daughter's life. It's hard to do anything before 3:00 PM though. I'm still sleeping when I get her at school."

He is a single father. He wants things to be different and has the resourcefulness to find a way, but he hasn't yet discovered the financial trick, as far as I know. Still, he always has a new phone and clean new sneakers.

"I get to work, and we do our stretches as a group. There are ten machines that do the whole process. There are two filters and the mask cutout and a six-point welder that welds the filter to the mask. Then I transfer it to the cut-and-seal machine, which cuts it out of the mold and seals the two layers of filter to the mold cutout. Then it goes to printing (another machine stamps on *Honeywell* and the day's date), and I inspect for holes and tears. Then to headbands and another welding machine, two on each side.

"It keeps me busy, but it's not hard work. It's the shift that's hard. How much work it is and the effect on my sleep patterns. But I'm doing something to help people. I'm making something. I'm finishing a product, start to finish. I'm out of the house. It's not fun unless you make it fun, which I do because I get to chop it with people, I get to socialize."

# RESPECT: RICHARD

"We clear trees. We use chain saws on long poles. We have the best equipment, every piece the best. The younger guys have no respect for the tools. When you use a chain saw, you clean it. You leave it filled with gas for the next guy. You put it back where you got it so the next guy can find it. They leave the place a pigsty."

# STUCK: DENNIS

"I just can't get to the water with my motor missing a piston. My friends text me, 'What, did you retire?'

"I used to have this badass, ten-thousand-buck motor. But owning a boat is a thousand bucks every time you go to the mechanic."

He looks at the floor. He's always had money trouble, as long as I've known him.

"How's your sleep?" I ask.

"My motor is weak. I don't want to get stuck."

I know he's stuck. His drinking doesn't help.

I think: *the full disaster.* But then I realize there might be worse yet for him.

# SOLITUDE: PEDRO

"I like the overnight shift. I like being alone. I go in at 2:00 AM. I pop the bagels in the oven. When they're ready, I dip them in toppings—onion, garlic. The croissants are next. Then the muffins. At 3:30 the donuts come in. The ones that don't have to be filled, I tray up. Last are the donuts that need to be filled and topped. I hand-frost and fill them with jelly or crème or apple and cinnamon or lemon. I put the trays in the showcase."

He has large brown eyes that can be read as either gentle or defeated.

"At 5:00 AM, I'm done and go home after the manager comes in. It's still dark. I go right to sleep. I'm up by 11:00, my kids already gone to school, my wife at work. I'm alone again."

# FLOORS: ELAINE

"I didn't have a name for six years. They just called me 'the girl.' Why was I so good? I just got down and did it."

Her hands are doughy, splotched with red telangiectasias.

"I didn't have a punch list, things to do the next day. It wasn't as if I never made a mistake, I just took care of it that day, unlike the men who carried the job over a day so they didn't have to work as hard. If I did the room, you *weren't* coming back the next day. I even did an operating room where you had to seal the floors perfectly so no germs could get in or out. You've got to know a lot of math."

She pauses to push a strand of her shoeshine-black hair behind her ear.

"A lot of rooms are not square. I'd measure out the shape of a room on red paper. I'd go into the other room where I had one large piece of linoleum and cut it out following the red paper. A single piece had to fit the room, no seams. Two-inch-thick linoleum where I had to take a blowtorch and heat the corners to flatten them down. I really didn't trust the straightedge; I could eyeball it better. It was a great workout. It was my artwork. To do twelve apartments and their utility closets, each one a different configuration—so many patterns!"

I look around at the corners of the office, and when she catches me checking out the handiwork, she gives a little laugh. It looks like a pretty good job to me.

"At the end of the day, I'd think: I did this. Look how beautiful this is.

"I was a girl, meticulous. The only girl floor installer in all my years."

# LOYALTY: MAUREEN

"I work in this nursing home. I help them get to the bathroom. I get them the breakfast menu. I do the laundry or clean or change bedsheets after an accident. One lady put me on workers' comp for two months. She was a little thing, maybe seventy pounds. She hit me with a shoe on the back of my head. She beat me with it. I wasn't allowed to put a hand on her, not even to stop her, and she had me cornered. If I touched her, I could get in trouble for abuse. The shoe was patent leather with a heel.

"My neck was sore for three months. The manager was worried I would sue, but I wasn't going to sue, I liked the job."

Shit jobs tend to be blue collar and paid by the hour, whereas bullshit jobs tend to be white collar and salaried.

—*Bullshit Jobs: A Theory*, David Graeber

## DARK SPACES: JEFFREY

"Not insulation; 'weathering' is the correct term. It doesn't take much skill, except making sure you don't fall through a ceiling, keeping your weight over the joists. But it's dirty and dusty work, crawling into dark spaces, that's why people don't want to do it."

He has a quick light voice, like none of what he says is very important.

"You're supposed to stop the job and crawl out of the attic if you see a bat, but I just tell my guys to look the other way and keep working. There are more bats in attics than you'd think. There are almost always mice. They don't mind the fiberglass; it probably keeps them warm. But they don't like the blown-in cellulose; it smells bad." He suppresses a laugh.

"You have to wear a mask, and it's hot in the summer, and it's careful work if you do it right, sealing the plates and every hole that a wire comes through, putting vent chutes in so the attic breathes. It's not really physical work, which is why I started going to the gym to get a workout. I'd rather do construction, but that doesn't pay as much."

# SHOW-OFF: JOE

"Lots of young guys are lazy. So I try to embarrass them. We pick the stop sign out of a concrete block, and there is cement hanging off it, and I pick up the sledgehammer to knock it off. They want to get the machine that punches it off, or they just sit in the truck, while I'm sixty-four years old and swinging the sledge."

His happiness is without excitement; it takes the form of a small drawn-out feeling of pride that lasts all day.

# UNDOUBTEDLY: LEO

"Why don't people like builders? They don't like interruption, invasion, trucks, dust. People doubt you. At the end of a project, you have a literal physical house. They can't doubt that. When someone can move into it, that's indisputable. That's rewarding. What drives me? The feeling of accomplishment. You work for six months and see it.

"I'm good at what I do, and it's difficult. I like wearing all the hats. I have to hire and to know prices and to build relations. Purchase land and go through approvals. Deal with police who come to the site to say you can't start until 8:00 AM. Excavation crews, attorneys, contractors, sales agents. Billings and insurance. I know a little about taxes. Getting dirty, landscaping, walkways. And I have to know how to sell it in the end.

"I'm a one-man band. I made a name for myself: he builds good homes."

# JOYSTICK: LUKE

"I sit in a machine all day—315 or 323 excavators. I dig in the ground, putting in water mains, new electrical upgrades, sewer lines, septic lines. I have a hoisting engineer license. I can tell you what's in the ground just by the feel of what's in my bucket. If we're getting near high-pressure line, or big rock, I can tell from the tension in the joystick. I can tell if the soil has been disturbed before. If I feel something's off, I send a ground guy to investigate, to hand-dig. Nothing going wrong makes me feel good."

He has tattoos on every finger besides his thumbs. His voice is loud enough to be heard over heavy machinery.

"The worst part is having to meet with people who think they know everything because they have a college degree. The best is the responsibility I get. Free rein. That's a sense of purpose right there.

"Being away from the family for a week can be bad. But I can't stand sitting at home. I get in trouble there. I've been with this company seven years, which is good because construction guys usually get laid off all the time."

## SKIN: KAT

"It doesn't really bother my hands because I use my body weight; you take one stance or another—archer, horse—and push with your legs. If I used only my hands all day, they'd be shot. Plus I make sure the table isn't too high for the effleurage—that's where you circle with your palm.

"Sometimes their skin is bad: boils, eczema, psoriasis. This one lady never let anyone see her naked except her husband, before me, and she had this creepy alligator skin, but I felt bad for her since her daughter died. I wear gloves if she bleeds. She chats and then drifts off to sleep; I love that. She wakes up and says she's thankful she met me."

She never says one word louder than another. She is peaceful. I can imagine a client falling asleep.

"I used to worry when I was younger that I had sweaty hands—hyperhidrosis they called it—but now I think of my hands as heat packs, and when I'm with clients they don't sweat much."

# FILLET: GENNARO

"I cut veal better than anyone who ever lived. I'd put myself up against anyone. I'm not saying this to be a wise guy, but I've seen a lot of people do it. It's the most difficult meat because it doesn't have stiffness or body like beef or pork. It's sloppy.

"Working with veal is fine knife-work. It's not a heavy cut through bone and muscle and gristle. You use a thin knife, like a sushi knife, that same weight and sharpness. It's about where you go into the meat to begin the procedure. Once you're in, the knife disappears and you have to ride the bone. Taking the bone out of a fifty-pound leg, where you give all the meat to the buyer, every piece that's theirs, without hacking anything off, no waste, that's the beauty."

His arms are deeply wrapped in muscle. He keeps them firmly folded across his chest. Much of life irritates him, but he smiles at the physical achievement of his work.

"It took me years. It's repetition. You don't realize how good you are until you hire someone and you work next to them, and it's like you're doing one thing and they're doing another."

## NO WAY: NICK

"The guys bust me when I do overtime. Don't you have a life? Why don't you go home? Overtime at your age? Tough times with the wife?

"But work gives me something to do.

"This guy comes up to me and says, 'They're buying out people. How old are you? You're close to retiring. You ought to take it.'

"I'm supposed to retire, and I don't want to. I don't know how to. What do I do if I retire early?"

More than one in three Americans belonged to a union in the 1950s; in 1983, one in five; by 2019, only one in ten. As union membership declined, income inequality rose.

## WHAT'S LEFT: DENNIS

"There are no clams left I hear. But I can't go by what people say."

I *only* go by what people say. A doctor's job consists of getting answers he doesn't expect.

"I might have to get a job. Amazon has a new warehouse opening. But I've never had a job before," he says with a little of both shame and surprise.

"You've had a job, a hard job," I say. "You just haven't had a boss." Or maybe clamming was such a pleasure he's never thought of it as a job.

In his blue hoodie, he looks at me carefully, my small eyes, my smile like a smirk.

"Your shirt's not tucked in," he says, smiling. Little does he know I wish I could dress like he does when he's working.

When I try to imagine another life besides clamming for him, I really can't.

"I've been my own boss, that's true. I'm my own digger."

Whenever he looks down, I can see that he's thinking.

# BLACKJACK: JAY

"I hated dealing cards. It was like being a robot. Most people think it's a good job. But pay isn't everything, and it didn't pay what people thought. People are not friendly when you take their money."

# COUNTER: KEVIN

"I work at a deli counter in a supermarket. You know the customers and what they want. It's a small place. My name tag fell off my hat, and they still knew my name.

"I work with nineteen-year-olds, college kids, so they disappear after a few months. They go to the bathroom nineteen times a day. They're in there hitting a Juul. They take advantage of being kids, though they want to be treated as adults. We got a toy Boar's Head football, and they are passing it down the aisle between customers."

He giggles. Age has come to him slowly. He still gets to the gym every day like a young man.

"I don't want to yell at them to the point where they won't listen. I'm good at it, letting them know the owner is watching on camera.

"I'm policing good kids."

He's got kids of his own at home—four girls under the age of ten. When we're not talking about his blood pressure, he keeps our conversations light. I'm not sure I would know if he was upset.

# KIDS' HELP: ANDRES

"I didn't want to be looked down on. I grew up poor, and I never wanted my kids to feel that. I never wanted them to know how we had to choose between paying the electric bill or for groceries. I had ideas—starting a landscaping business or doing roof slating. But I had to bring in income.

"I didn't have a shot. I would think: I can change the arc of my life."

Sometimes when patients start talking, I find myself tucking my new shoes deeper under my chair.

"Nowadays, if I was fired tomorrow, I could pay bills for six months. But I'm still worried about retirement, and I don't want my kids to help."

# UNSOCIAL CLIMBER: NELSON

"I painted water towers. I had three forty-foot ladders connected by a cable to get me to the top of the water sphere that had to get spruced up. I banged the tank when I had to move, and the guys on the ground moved the ladders. I knew tricks, like priming with paint from the ground by shooting paint-covered balls rather than going up there.

"I liked testing myself. One hundred fifty feet up. I'm the one laying on the ladder, painting. I liked the hero thing. I knew it would be hard for some people. I was like Spiderman."

He is a large man, but his hands are enormous. I imagine him with suction cups at the fingertips.

"It was great money, but it was crazy, I think. I got a lot of work; people begged me because no one else wanted to do it."

# WEEKENDS: CLINTON

"Coming into the job at the factory, I was mechanically inclined. I always liked to weld and learn motors. I like the guys who work there; they're like car guys—interested in engines, trucks with superchargers—acting like kids, talking about cars all day. I install molds, do preventative maintenance on equipment. I work with the site manager to determine which products need priority. This job helps me put another notch in my record."

I catch myself admiring his ambition.

"I always get called back for overtime. I hate that there's never a happy medium. I hate the production schedule. My last forty-hour week was eight years ago. I like the money, but I like my weekends better."

# RESTAURANTS: NOLAN

"I have this manager who is always on the same shift as me and doesn't treat me fairly. He gives everyone a table but won't seat people in my section. He's rude. 'I don't want to look at you,' he says. Then he repackages his insult, makes it sound less aggressive. 'I don't want to see anyone.'"

He is used to being insulted. He takes blame for his collapses but not his achievements.

"It's a good ADHD environment though. You can't think about things. You work constantly. It's chaotic, but I flourish. My brain is a restaurant; it works that way—busy."

He is smiling, an unusual display of emotion for him, but he seems very pleased with his metaphor.

# 2

# LOSSES

I have many patients who work dangerous jobs, or make them more dangerous with their impatience with coworkers and onerous safety protocols. They get hurt. They fall from heights. Machines tear into them. Too many are philosophical about their injuries: "Nobody gives you nothing for free," one said recently. Pain is the price of working. Work, like gin, dims pain, Joan Didion once said.

And when there is no work, pain reappears. Alan Krueger, chair of President Obama's Council of Economic Advisers, calculated in 2017 that nearly half of all nonworking men were taking pain medication on a daily basis and argued that the increased prescribing of opioids could explain a lot of the decline in the male labor force.

Sometimes I ask patients: Has your work affected your health in the past for better or for worse? They rarely think about whether work makes them healthier, but they can cite every instance when it has made them unhealthier. They have bursitis and tendinitis and are exposed to toxic chemicals. Employers smell the roses, but the workers get the thorns, one once told me. But what is clear to me is that work changes people. Work can physically debilitate, sure, but it can also change patients' mental experience of the world and of themselves. ADHD, depression, OCD are all helped by work that requires attention, that serves as a kind of coping. I once cared for a dressmaker whose craft required constant practice, and such practice made her less anxious, so when she stopped working, she grew scared and hesitant and barely left her house. Paychecks too can push away anxiety, at least for a time. I've seen patients quit using drugs to keep a job. Work can cure self-centeredness and restlessness. Unconsciously, many know the benefits of working: they find jobs that suit them or match their mental or physical disabilities. My patient who's a loner works the third shift at a donut shop; my patient with a phlebitic, swollen leg takes a job where she can sit down. Work can provide a therapeutic transformation. Indeed, therapeutic communities for people recovering from addiction are all about work as a form of structure, but also a belief and a practice and a responsibility.

My sense is that people generally like to work, and denying a person permission to work while at the same time reproaching them for idleness (this happens all the time to people who have served prison time and have felony records) is a conceptually flawed construction. For poverty hardliners, even the right to a place in heaven is predicated on work. So when my patients can't work due to illness or injury, I sign forms for temporary disability so that they get paid time at home. Illness can be an excuse not to work, but a job site as a place to ignore illness did not serve public health well during COVID-19. I sign doctor-visit and out-of-work notes for employers, adding a few extra days when patients ask. I have the power to give people a break from their work lives and some of their money worries. But staying home with kids or parents—its own unpaid work, feminism's forgotten fight—has other demands, and many are only too glad to leave the house again.

No one questions the value of work, but perhaps we underestimate its value. Having seen patients for so long, and having read the literature on this subject, I know that being employed is associated with better health. Good jobs are protective of health, bad jobs are not. Working does not bring health, but not working wears us down. Research has shown that regions where plant closures and job losses have eroded long-standing paths to a good life are the areas where people are now sickest.

# ONLY HOPE: DENNIS

"I haven't had the bottom of the boat cleaned," he starts today.

Last time he said he couldn't afford to get his piston fixed after a year. Each visit now he has a list of excuses for not working.

"No Amazon?" I ask. He hasn't brought up the warehouse job possibility again.

"It's depressing when I'm not on a boat."

I'm surprised to hear him use the word *depressing*. I hear about his being behind on child support payments for the two daughters whom he rarely sees but speaks with on the phone weekly and affectionately, a new woman he's chasing who works in a bar and won't call him back, being evicted from his house and now sharing an apartment with a buddy, vodka nips in the morning to steady himself.

He's never seemed to notice all the losses before. Or said them to me, at least.

He wouldn't deny it: he loved clamming more than any of his other attachments. Which perhaps is his only hope to stop drinking and get back to work.

# UNREPENTANT: MICHELLE

"My McDonald's shift is 6:00 PM to 1:00 AM. I went to school with the owner's ex-husband, and he was my pot dealer; that's how I got the job."

She never smiles much. But she's never seemed aggravated by the work she's been given.

"Then a laptop went missing. I bring my shoes to work in a backpack, and I carry a big purse, so she figured I had a way to sneak it out. She told everyone I stole it, and she fired me. I didn't touch it.

"Then a sixteen-year-old who worked there called and told her he took it and brought it back. He worked that night.

"She had someone else call to tell me I had my job back."

# WAITING: DEB

"I lost my job when my fingers swelled up. Nothing works in my hands anymore. It takes two hands to hold coffee, and my fingers are still cold. I go to bed with mittens. I don't sleep for days at a time."

With her rheumatoid, she can't fully straighten her fingers, the joints are so inflamed.

"As much as I couldn't stand my boss, I miss the work. It was something to do, liking a few people, a paycheck of course. I kept busy. Now I'm bored. My brain stops working. Sometimes I want to hurry up and die, get it over with; it's going to happen."

The United States alone among peer nations has no guaranteed maternity leave and no legal right to sick leave or vacation time.

## INNOCENT MISTAKE: LAMSON

"I was wearing my friend's jacket, and there was pot in the pocket. I didn't know what it was—I was a kid—but someone rolled it and I tried it. I smoked half. We got raided in the hotel room, all of us under twenty-five on a job out of town. The boss left my final check thumbtacked to the bulletin board with a note: *Don't come back.*"

## THE SYSTEM: CARIN

"I get a call from the unemployment office after I file online. The guy asks, 'Why were you laid off?'

"I say to him, 'I was told by my manager that my services were no longer needed.' When I asked why, my boss says, 'I was told I can't put you on the schedule.' 'That's not a reason,' I say.'"

"No, it's not," I say. I feel defeated by her exchange with her boss; I can imagine how she felt.

"The unemployment guy tells me he'll call me in forty-eight hours after he talks to my employer. If my employer answers the phone, I'll probably get my money—$160 a week, he says. If my employer tells some other story and says there was a reason I needed to be fired, maybe I won't get my money, he says.

"This guy at the unemployment office decides. I don't know how he decides."

She is baffled, and unprepared to be out of work.

# ENOUGH: WALTER

"I've been getting up at the crack of dawn since I was eighteen doing this factory work. I'll never be able to fully retire, but I might be able to cut back to fifteen or twenty hours a week."

I am surprised to find myself not especially sure of what to say. He is my age and looks older. His hands, gentle on his lap, twitch. I wonder: *Is escape something he dreams of?*

"I'll have to find another job somewhere, but I'll have a small pension from this one, and social security and that will be enough."

## DISAPPOINTMENTS: STEVEN

"In the winter, I'd stand by the window when I was a kid and wait for the flakes. 'Here they come,' I'd yell. The plows would go by, and I'd run to open the front door. I always wanted to drive big trucks—backhoes, gravel diggers, dump trucks; I never did, but I do have my plow. I still get excited, even at forty-seven years old.

"It's a tough job. You sit there in your cab for thirteen hours. Zero visibility. Cars going by that you don't want to hit. It's no joke. You have to have a clear brain. The worst day of my life was when my boss smelled booze on me and said, 'What are you doing?' I was a subcontractor, and he loved me to death because I was a hard worker and never made up fake hours. I'm honest. But he had to let me go."

# CAN'T: JOANNE

"I live in subsidized housing. I supported myself from eighteen until I was forty-four, when I had a breakdown. I know people in my building who should work and don't. There's a young guy who drives a good car. He claims he can't speak English, though I heard him. Physically, there's nothing wrong with him that I can see."

She pauses. She watches me warily. I can hear the shuffling of feet outside the door in the hall.

"Some of my neighbors probably think the same about me."

Sometimes doctoring is figuring out when you don't understand something but know it's the wrong time to ask a question.

# CLOSE: ANGELINE

"I lost the job because I got close to the other women who worked there and told them I was trans, and they told the boss that they were uncomfortable in the bathroom with me.

"After that I was paranoid. I was afraid to leave the house. Someone would jump me. I got SSI for being diagnosed bipolar. I never worked again."

I know she stays at home mostly, watching old TV reruns. I am glad to know she has a sister she is close with and a few friends in the building.

# RAISE: GAYLE

"I recommend a friend to come cook where I do. She makes $14 an hour to start, and I make $16.50. After ninety days, they raise her to $17. Nothing against her, and she should take what they offer, but that's more than I make after five years."

Her fingers are red, boiled. Her voice is garbled with emotion.

"I complain to my boss and then to the district manager and then to the owner of the company. He says, 'You'll have to wait until the next review in January to get a raise.' I ask how she can make more after ninety days and didn't have to wait until January, and he says, 'We give raises based on performance and not seniority.' I say, 'Well, from now on you get my performance only one day a week rather than four.'"

# THE OLD MAN: DENNIS

After hearing him admit to being depressed at his last visit, I welcome him in from the waiting area and make much of his coming back to see me, never an easy task for a patient.

"If you're not clamming, you're not making money, so how are you getting along?" I ask. I feel like he hasn't quite given me the full story. For some reason, I'm invested in getting him back in his boat. What I also want to ask is: What would it take to get you out there? An antidepressant? A few days in detox? It would be better if he simply stopped drinking, but that seems impossible.

"I'm doing okay," he says. "I'm taking care of the old man. Hardest job I ever had." There's a kind of sweetness in his tone, like I've never heard before. "I started living with him and his son, who was a friend of mine, when my mom put me out because we were arguing. Three weeks in, my friend died of a heart attack. I stayed on because I needed a place to stay. But then I started to like it.

"I take care of the old man rent-free. He's eighty-seven and had a stroke and can't move his left arm or leg. I get him out of bed. I put him on the toilet, grocery shop, cook three meals, feed him, clean the house. He sits at the window and looks out at the garden where he had 250 tomato plants in his day, but hasn't in years, and he talks my ear off about fishing and politics. I don't want to leave him alone, in case he falls trying to get up, so I just hang out with him all day, and I watch TV and drink.

"You know, I worked in a nursing home when I was sixteen. I'd bring coffee and set up the silverware for the old people at Cedarcrest every morning. I'd quit school, and I thought making money was everything because I was building a hot rod, this antique Oldsmobile Cutlass. I sold it when I lost my license.

"At twenty, I bought a house and a wedding band, and five years later I was divorced. This is the first time since then that I'm living in a house instead of an apartment."

I'm disappointed that he's settled into this caregiver's life; I won't deny it. It's not hard to explain. I remember that bursting feeling of success—for him and for me—when he would come into my office with a burlap bag stuffed with fifty clams for my dinner that night.

## UP IN THE AIR: NORMAN

"Before I went into the military, I grew up doing construction, building tall buildings. Up off the ground, walking around two-by-sixes didn't bother me at all. And that was my plan when I got out."

He is easily distracted, turning toward every sound outside the door.

"But when I got out of the service, I don't know if it was because of the anxiety or whatever, but once I got up over ten feet, got up to twenty feet in the air, where I used to just walk along and do my work, I couldn't do it."

With certain people I am less at ease. I understand that my optimism is sometimes an illusion, that life is headed toward a fall.

One quarter
of those staying
in homeless
shelters have jobs.

## LIMITS: DARRELL

"My unemployment ran out. So I'm looking for a job again. Looking for anything. If I didn't have a felony record, I wouldn't have to do only shit work, kitchen work. I know restaurants. I have fifteen years' experience at fine dining. Half my life doing it. Followed my brother into it, and I'm proud of that, but it's the same every day.

"I want landscaping, lawns and gardens. I got a business card made."

# SUITED: JUSTIN

"We made the best suiting fabric. It was an employee-owned company. I started on the looms, running the machine, inspecting the products, checking them against the master swath. My group respected me, looked to me as a boss. I was honest, not afraid to admit to a mistake."

He has an ex-Marine sergeant's sense of duty. His emotional alertness always moves, surprises, impresses me.

"I'd treat people mostly the same, though everyone is not the same. A lot of Laotians worked there, and they knew I had no biases. I was in charge of four hundred people in my thirties. Then the company folded."

## SELF-EMPLOYED: KEITH

"I really just want to work for myself. I'm a great worker, but I'm not reliable for a job. I have a bout of depression, don't show up, and I'm fired. I'm reliable to myself though."

## NEVER NOT: NOAH

"My mood swings would fluctuate quite frequently. I couldn't concentrate on my work; I was not dependable. And I've never *not* been dependable in my entire life.

"When I got to the point where I wouldn't even hire myself, because maybe I'd be there a half a day—in the morning or in the afternoon, who knows?—because of the confusion of my head, the memory loss, just not remembering to do stuff, I just shut down. I quit. It's humiliating for a person like me."

"But it's hard to get along with people during kitchen madness. I keep cool as the work gets crazy."

She lasts maybe two weeks at these kitchen jobs and then shows up late a few times. She gets a warning—and then doesn't show up at all.

# BY THE WAY: THOMAS

"It's not easy to say, 'Oh, by the way, I have PTSD and traumatic brain injury and all this stuff.' It's not an easy thing to tell a prospective employer. To this guy who doesn't know me."

He has cracked palms and a grimace of utter desperation. He moves his eyes slowly left and then slowly right.

"And if I get the job, I know what's going to happen. When someone goes on with the conversation too long, and they're trying to get a point through, I'll have to stop them.

"Then they'll get mad because I can't get through the whole thing I'm trying to say because I've lost the beginning by the end. They don't understand it, and they just get pissed."

Even with me, he is cut off, out of contact, beyond reach.

## AT LEAST: SHANNON

"I did Avon. I painted key chains. I worked with medical supplies, putting catheters in bags. Never liked any of those jobs. Hairdressing school neither. I didn't stick with it because I didn't have a car. I'd rather stay home with kids."

She spins her hair around her finger.

"But I never got fired."

# LIFE DECISIONS: LORI

"I started at the jewelry store when I was pregnant. I worked very hard. I got raises here and there. I made enough to get an apartment. Then my boss asks me if I've been working overtime because she's short on her budget. I asked her: 'Did you factor in my raise?' She says, 'What raise? It was a glitch in the pay system.' She takes it away."

Something in her face is hardening now that she says it out loud.

"I tell her I made life decisions based on my raise. 'You can't just do this to me,' I say. 'That's not right. Let's meet halfway at least.'

"They let me go for complaining. I vowed never to work for a big company again. I went back to bartending."

# OFF: TARA

She is sitting at the desk next to the sink when I come into the room.

"You asked me about what I do for a living last time, and I didn't answer you."

She doesn't make much eye contact.

"I don't work because I'm unbalanced. Anything to do with reading, I can't do it. I can't write either. I've tried to commit suicide three times."

She sets her two arms like L's on the desktop in front of her and puts her head down on them.

## INSIDE OUT: VANCE

"I used to weld standing inside giant pipes and tanks. Now, every new place I go I'm thinking: What do I do if I'm in a room and you can't get out? Sometimes I have to leave; I've got to get outside. What happens if I can't get out? If the elevator doesn't work when I'm inside it? I used to think anxiety was a joke."

He's filled with irrefutable insights. I finally understand why the exam room door is always slightly ajar when I arrive at the room he's in.

"Now I'm afraid to get on a plane or go to a concert."

In 1979 there were twenty million manufacturing jobs in the U.S., and now there are twelve million when the population is 50 percent larger.

## NINE LIVES: TERENCE

"I been read the last rites nine times."

I give a little nervous laugh before even deciding what to say. "That doesn't sound good."

"There was the time I tried to jump on the back of a moving truck and missed. But mostly it's been industrial accidents. The last one I was working in a gravel yard loading gravel onto a conveyor belt. One day the belt was off, and I told the oiler it needed to be fixed, but the man wouldn't do it. So I went up and greased the rollers myself, and when I was on the ladder the belt snapped and wrapped me up and took me into the metal."

I want to know where he's working now, but I'm afraid to ask.

# 3.

# CONNECTIONS

Sometimes a parent teaches their child to do the work they do, which is a way of teaching about themselves. Sometimes parents draw their children into their line of work because it is gratifying. Research has also shown that physically demanding work often leads to greater job satisfaction—irrespective of how well it is paid. Many of those working in harsh conditions doing tough manual labor or apparently unpleasant jobs actually find it rewarding, even when it is not highly valued monetarily. This goes some way toward explaining why firefighters, operating engineers (driving tractors, bulldozers, backhoes), and construction workers are among the happiest jobs, and why the children of firefighters often become firefighters, why contractors train their children and go into business with them.

It's interesting to compare these favored jobs with the list of the most hated jobs (such as director of information technology, director of sales and marketing, and senior web developer), which are generally much better paying and have higher social status. What's striking about the list is that these relatively high-level corporate workers often feel imprisoned in hierarchical bureaucracies. They see little point in what they are doing.

Everybody carries to work what they got from home, from their culture, their community, the family they grew up in. Upbringing is an invisible force underneath all of the manifest dynamics that take place at work. Family defines how you ask for help, how you trust others, how you own up to your mistakes.

Trust and vulnerability, the vocabulary of emotions, conflict and exploitation—all are different when a patient of mine works with family or a close friend. Everything is up for conversation, everything is a negotiation. There is a second and different level of work happening: the emotional labor of listening.

Working with family erodes work-life balance. Can you ask relatives to work anytime you want, at 9:00 at night, because there should be no boundaries when working with family? Does it mean that they should care about the company as if it were theirs, even though their name is not yet on the side of the truck? Does it mean you can demand a level of loyalty because they're family? It is often unclear what working with and for family entitles you to and what it might demand from you. Working with family may mean working in a highly intrusive workplace. Sometimes it may mean that people are constantly backbiting. Sometimes there is intense solidarity. Every workplace has a hierarchy; every family has a power structure.

Work is a force that shapes identity and provides connection and security, whether you are working in a family business or with people you barely know. It is difficult to sustain and grow an intergenerational family business. When businesses fail, family bonds can be broken. Sometimes it's better to work alone.

# QUAHOG: DENNIS

"The old man kind of reminds me of my grandfather," he says. "I used to go quahogging with my grandfather at the end of the road where we lived. We'd find clams between the rocks. My stepfather gave me his boat to get me started."

Before I moved to this part of the country, I didn't know that a quahog was a kind of clam. Hard shell. Round. Chopped into chowder.

"He was an Alaskan fisherman. He was one of two survivors of a boat that went down, and he moved here. When he gave me his old boat, I didn't plan to do this for my life.

"He always used to say quahogging is not a good full-time job. 'Maybe weekends,' he said."

"Really?" I say with astonishment. "But you've done it full-time for your whole life until recently."

I assume he would want to provide an explanation, but he does not.

These rooms I've gotten to know are all filled to the brim with ghosts.

# FAMILY NAME: ERAN

"We make the electrical contacts for cars, soldering onto glass—you know, for defoggers, brake lights. I make a spray flux to help the solder adhere to the glass. The silver's embedded in glass, but it needs a connector wire and a clip.

"I go around and support the girls doing the work. I set up the new machines, I get an old machine running again, you know. Or if they need more wire, or more connectors. I do a little of everything, you know. That makes the days go faster, you know."

He is a bit of a mechanical genius, one of those people who can fix anything.

"It's a family business; my father started it in 1948. He originally made jewelry—religious beads, saint medals. My name is on the building."

I can see it matters very much to him.

## HUMILIATIONS: DOMINIC

"My father sold the business to my brother behind my back. The three of us worked together selling fish until my father went to Florida because he wanted ten years off, he said. We still sent him $2,000 a week. Green. No taxes. We had to make $3,500 to clear that. Plus we paid him $30,000 for the inventory before he left.

"From almost the beginning, my brother had been telling my father that I wasn't around, wasn't really working anymore, I found out later. My father gets back to town the ninth year, and the daily humiliations from my brother began. Like I'd ask one of the employees to do something, and my brother would come out and say to the worker, 'Who asked you to do that? You don't have to do that.'

"They thought it would be easier if I quit, but I wouldn't, so my brother fired me, and my father gave him the keys to the store. Really, my brother's wife didn't want me around. She wanted the money for herself.

"I had to sell my house, got divorced, lost my kids, and I haven't worked a day since. I loved that store."

## PAINT BY NUMBERS: CARLOS

"Sometimes I paint with my brother-in-law's company, although he pays less than I can get elsewhere. We were painting this three-story square house the other day, and no one in his crew wants to go up and paint the window frames on the third floor. I was the only one. If those frames weren't completed, the job wasn't complete. I took the risk. I never agreed when I signed on that I would do the high work, by hand, at the top of the ladder in the heat.

"After, I said to my brother-in-law, 'I made it so that you didn't have to go up there yourself. I did it willingly. But I did it. I should be paid more for that.' But he wouldn't; he wants more for himself. My sister, I love her to death, but she's in the business too, and I have to think she was in on the decision not to pay me extra. What I don't get goes into her pocket too."

# DESERVING: FRANK

"My father won't work with me. We're in the same business, building houses. I worked for him since I was a kid, sweeping up on his job sites. It hurts my reputation when he goes into business now with guys who used to work for me. They must look at me and say behind my back, 'I wonder why his father is working with us and not him?'"

I can see that he is uncomfortable with resentment, but he isn't inclined to open up.

"It's always a 'maybe' from him, but never a job. His latest reason is, 'We do things differently.'

"I'm good at what I do. I have the respect of my crew. Guys who work for me show up. My father said, 'Do it yourself,' and I did for a decade, *successfully*. I deserve to get a chance to work with him now; it's the next step in my career, bigger jobs. But I'm not going to 'play son' anymore. There's nothing new except his excuses. I don't get it."

## STREAKS: JOSH

"It was my mother's car wash. When I worked there, I was the only person speaking English. The worst was in the winter, trying to get snow out of the wheel wells. The power washer didn't work. You had to turn it around and poke it like a pool stick. Some people forget to put their car in neutral when they pull onto the track, which means when it comes out the other end, I would have to jump into the front seat of a moving car to save it from running off.

"Wiping the windows of three hundred cars when you're not good at it wasn't fun either. I never figured out that circular motion. I'd leave streaks.

"I had the idea of making money from detailing the inside of cars, and I charged $250 and hired this guy to do it and paid him $50 until my mother found out I was keeping the money and fired me for a week. She was tough. When I got back, she had hired someone herself to do the detailing."

# STAY AWAY: BRENDAN

“I take forty hours a week at Burger King, even though I’m only allowed twenty as a high school student.”

He is all edges, and lank, an apparition from a famine. His face is old, a deep vertical line between his eyebrows.

“I work so that I can be out of the house. So I don’t have to see my stepfather, so I don’t hit him in the face or push him down the stairs. Working is easier than worrying about getting arrested.”

# GETTING ALONG: CONOR

"My teachers used to tell my father, 'Every time your son has a writing assignment, he writes about you and heating systems.' I was mechanical to begin with—I took apart everything when I was a kid to see how it worked. And I always got along with my father. Now we work together. Although I guess to the government, I technically work *for* him. But I tell him what he's doing wrong about as often as he tells me what I'm doing wrong. I'll say to him, 'You taped that backward,' and he'll say, 'No I didn't.'

"Most people don't care that much about the company they work for, but I'll take over the business eventually. You got to want to be successful to do this. People need you, and you have to show up in an emergency; you can't shut your phone off. Ever. He will never retire though. My mother says, 'He'll work until he drops.'"

# TOO MUCH INFORMATION: ROLAND

"The worst part of my job is the gossip."

He shakes his head, an antisocial man who needs people.

"I never seen guys gossip so much. We know everyone's business. Bob's leaving? We know his pension, that he converts his paycheck to coins and buries them in his yard, that after his wife died—terrible—he's been living with his two sisters-in-law, and they are trying to poison him. You'd think grown men, truck drivers, wouldn't be as interested in the stories, but they are."

# FRAMES: STEVE

"My father is a whiz with a sewing machine. I started at twelve, working with my father. He used to fix rips in vinyl and then realized there was better-paying work in upholstery, so he hired an Italian seamstress to teach him. He was working for this furniture store, and I was with him one day when I was about twenty and we heard the salesmen talking causally about 'no fits,' the couches they sold that didn't fit into the door frames of these little city apartments. I thought: Why not take the sofa apart and put it together inside the apartment?

"I'm good with the frame. You learn the shape of sofas from upholstery, but I also learned about the joints. And then I learned about the Sawzal, this reciprocating saw that cuts frames. The good sofas are all about the wood—hardwood shaped by hand, not what comes off assembly lines. Anyway, I guess I just had an eye for it.

"I wish I was rich, and I'd rather have been a nurse or a hairdresser like my sister, but I suppose of all the people who know frames, I have a specialty: springs. Under the foam you sit on, you need spring tension. There are eight ways to tie down or compress a steel spring to give it tension. I tie it with Italian twine. Look at me: rope burns on my hands. I'm the best at it, and I couldn't care about it at all. It's a job. That's just what I do, and I've stuck with it."

## SELF-RELIANCE: DILLON

"I hunt some and farm more. My wife is an equal partner. She weeds and harvests. She does the kitchen work, canning, pickling, freezing. To the extent that we can, we live off the land. We grow vegetables organically, mostly organically, if not by the book. We raise chickens. I barter with the dairy man down the road."

He plucks at the skin on the back of his hand as if he wants to pull off the annoying husk.

## ENGINE EAR: ROBIN

"Working on a car you gotta think and know things. I could have been working in the office or on the books in my father's garage, but I like to be smart; anyone can type. It's hard to read blueprints and know math.

"My father's favorite line to me was 'Go figure it out.' Pull that alternator out, take it apart, and rebuild it, that's how you learn. I had to put it together again.

"The hardest work in cars is the electrical part, and that's what my father specialized in. If your window didn't go down or your blinker didn't work. You learn sounds. If you start the car and it goes tick tick, it's the solenoid. If it scrapes, it's the coil."

# BUTCHER: MICHAEL

"I thought the best bet for me was in the family business. When I was young, I would work in the front of the store, selling. I liked hearing one customer say to the other, 'Whatever that kid says, do it.' But I was raised to believe I was an idiot."

I remember how in the butcher shop of my childhood the white paper that wrapped the meat was ripped to size over a toothed, metal bar.

"I thought, later in life, when I took it over, I'd make some money. My father paid me and everyone else lousy.

"I had pride in my ability, skinning the product, how many pounds I could get, beginning to end. I was faster, more precise. I got more meat with less waste. I could butterfly with an even thickness. I could glide my knife like a machine."

# MAYBE BETTER: DENNIS

"The old man died a few weeks back. I wasn't expecting it. I was talking to him fine the day before, and then he didn't wake up.

"I went back to live with my mother. My mother's been taking drugs since her knee was done, even though she doesn't need them. She's a negative person. I drink, and we get going at each other. Now she wants me out. She did a 360 on me.

"Now I stay in my room and keep my mouth shut since I don't have the cash to leave. She's a clean freak like I am. I see where it comes from. I see her self-pity in me. But I've got to change it in myself."

I am surprised by the vehemence in his voice. He's got more energy than I've heard in months.

"I have a shot at getting a cheaper motor. Bigger. Maybe better. A 225 Yamaha."

"That sounds good," I say with gusto, enthusiasm. I give him a thumbs-up.

Half of those
who patronize food
banks live in
a household with a
full-time worker.

## BOILERS: BILL

"I finished high school and went to trade school. My girlfriend was pregnant. I was ready to go to the Air Force, but she objected. I had a friend who was a diesel mechanic, and he got me a job working boilers.

"I do installs: propane, boilers, generators. You need a basic understanding of electricity—control, wiring, operating mechanism, proving switches, relays. I like getting people heat or air conditioning; I find that satisfying. I like that accomplishment each time. I hate the cleaning, vacuuming, changing filters—that's just monotonous. I prefer the puzzles, the challenges."

He trails off, looking pleased.

"My dad was a boiler attendant in the Navy, but he never showed me a thing. He worked at the VA and Navy, but never residential. Still, he liked it when I got my master license."

## COMPETITION: ERIC

"I do painting, anything I can handle myself. I haven't gotten new business recently, but old customers are helping me, asking me to paint a living room here, a ceiling there.

"We got divorced because she kept asking, 'You going to work today?' She saw I couldn't build a business."

I look away to give him a moment of privacy.

"You gotta know somebody to get the job. Otherwise, there's competition from everyone. Even landscapers now say they can paint your house."

# BUSTED: JACK

"I feel part of a brotherhood. When another Amtrak truck passes, we wave. We're part of a brotherhood, risking our lives to help others."

One of his fingers is deformed, flattened at the tip. His left knee is crooked. I've never heard him complain.

"I replace the ties, the timber ties that sit under the train track. We're out on a bridge. It's a bunch of guys working together, like we're building a house. You take the track off the old ties—they wear out—get the old timber, and throw it onto a wagon. Take out the new ties. Other guys attach the track to the ties by J-hook. Without us, they can't do their work; without them, we can't do ours."

# SOLES: THEO

"My father opened the shoe repair, the size of a closet. On summers off from school, I'd go to work with him—there was no babysitting then, and I'd work at the shoeshine stand inside the shop. At sixteen, I started to peel off heels and soles, and he showed me how to grind. He never let me do stitching; there was a big clunky machine that was dangerous. I enjoyed killing time there; I was excited to do something. I'd get my father coffee. I took over when he got dementia. I had wanted to buy a pizza shop, but that was too many hours."

He has a long, drooping black mustache. I think: Only afterwards a person looks back and sees where he was heading.

"Shoes would come in a wooden form, and I'd add the welt with a welting machine, the perimeter, then the sole on the welt, then I'd stitch because the glues were less strong than today. I liked to interact with people. It was a good living, but now the prices of materials are too high. A repair used to cost one-third in material; now it's half.

"I pay no rent because I moved the shop to the basement of my mother's building. I have grinding and shaping machines. It's a pretty simplistic business, not rocket science. The glues change, and how you lay it; the shoe and boot materials change, the bonds change, but the fundamentals are the same. The job never disappoints me.

"I never advertise, all word of mouth. If you like my work, you come back. I'm courteous and give good service, but I never say I'm perfect. Now my mother brings me coffee."

# QUITS: EARLE

"I was styling director for Bloomingdale's. I loved what I did; I would have done it for nothing—travel, pretty girls. I was one of those people who could do drugs and work just fine.

"I was doing well when my mother got sick. My father didn't want to be around my mother, and I realized later it was because he was scared. I just thought he was mean, but he didn't know how to deal. You need someone twenty-four hours a day when you have Alzheimer's, so I quit my job to take care of her.

"When she died, he got sick, and I took care of him. I never went back to styling."

## OLD SCHOOL: VLAD

"I'm a cook, but I have a food safety license too. I took a course, which makes me valuable, since at every restaurant there has to be at least one person there at any given time with a license.

"My mother cooked at home and in a restaurant for thirty years, so I'm capable and good at it too."

His features are so gaunt, they give the impression of undernourishment, but when he talks about food and his mother, the hard lines of his face relax and his cheeks fill out.

"The old-school chefs, like my mother, what they do with very little is amazing. Anyone can buy a tenderloin and make it tender. But if you buy tough meat, braising it gets you the best flavor and greatest tenderness. That's what my mother taught me."

# PATERNITY: AVELINO

"Unemployment is nice at first. But then it's devastating because I know I'm not setting an example for my kids.

"My mother begged my father to go to work, but because he was an alcoholic, he didn't. I don't want my kids to see that."

I can tell he is in some form of competition with his father, and that he's winning.

"When I lose one job, I know I'll get another."

Employees can be denied sick leave if their employers determine that they do not need them to work; no documentation is required to justify the employer's decision.

# REALIZATION: DONALD

"Most of my life I was hand to mouth. You never have enough when you have kids. I had four, and I was buying diapers again after fifteen years.

"The first time I was laid off I was a young father married four years. My wife was a bank teller. I worried how I'd keep things going. My wife took a waitressing job without telling me. She'd gone to private school, and I never thought of her as someone who'd wait tables. The day I found out, I realized what a partner she was and how much I loved her."

# 4

# SURVIVAL

The people I care for, with and without medical insurance, are "working class." But what defines a working-class life? The way you live, the amount of money you make, or the nature of the work, the culture you are part of? To many, working class means simply *not poor*. Still, most people who come to me need extra cash, more income.

If you ask people why they work, most will say, "For the money." But at work they make friends, exert power, avoid certain people, discuss lunch, pass the time, get bored, resist bosses, stay late, study new techniques, talk about winning the lottery, plan for the next job. They also work for routine, for ritual, to be part of something greater than themselves, or part of a community. Works defines them socially. They mostly are conscientious and want to do well.

But every one of my patients waits for that paycheck. They work for recognition, for a sense of peace, for astonishment. But they spend every dollar of their weekly wage. Work offers a place where they can be decisive, or rude and raucous. Working with one's hands is being good at the discipline of managing unforgiving, demanding materials. Repetitive motions with slight adjustments offer the pleasures of procedural thinking. Learning through the body. These are not small pleasures.

**MY PATIENTS ARE SURPRISED AT** the end of a day of pouring a driveway's concrete by how it's gone; it took longer than expected and turned out better than imagined. Today's task is done by moving forward, inch by inch, meter by meter, until the hard work is done—the fountain moved, the third floor painted, the counter installed. But they often take second jobs. Sometimes they work sixteen hours a day, which is like working two jobs. Sometimes the only thing they like is clocking out at the end of a shift. Nobody faults the cleaners of public restrooms for looking forward to the end of the day or to a time when they can have better work. Some hate their jobs and can't wait to get to a bar right after. They hate smelling like turpentine or fish when they get home. They strip off dirty clothes before going into the house. Sometimes what's hard about the work is that they can't walk away from it at night—the day's mistakes stay with them—or have to go back to it on the weekend. To "earn a living" is an abominable expression, although I suppose it gets at the idea of money that's needed but also deserved after a long day. The phrase "to make a living" I suppose gets at the hardship of working. I've certainly seen that you can work at the expense of living.

**MAYBE MEDICINE IS A CALLING,** but graduating from medical school offered me capitalism's luxury of choice: this kind of doctor or that, procedures or hands, the latter used only to detect and diagnose, feeling for new patterns of damage. It took me some time to understand that I live and work in the realm of privilege. Everything has been given to me: education, social ease, money, thanks to which I've been able to choose my life freely and do what I like, pretty much as I please. I write books and see patients. They live in the world of tight budgets. Saying to me, "I collect garbage," or "I work the third shift as a nursing aide," is like saying, "I didn't get to choose. I have to earn my living. I am subject to the laws of necessity." Not everyone has work choices. For some, deeply meaningful work is not an option; minimum wages rarely offer this scenario.

In 1974, when Studs Terkel travelled America talking to workers about what they did all day, wages were at the highest in US history following the post–World War II boom. Wages have since gone down (except for a brief bump up during COVID-19 when essential work was recognized as worth the price), and work has become insecure again.

In my book *Broke*, where patients spoke to me about money (and their lack of it) and inevitably about their jobs, work was accomplished in the midst of other demands. Even without a job, patients of mine would still have plenty to do. They would have housework and yard work, work to do on their cars, and the work of childcare. Paid work gets in the way of these types of work. While they might work for a sense of fulfillment and the rewards of the work itself, for the people I see, work is about money, making enough that they can feel safe enough that they can take some things for granted—food, shelter. Work is not political, not about seizing the means of production, but about getting by. Toil is the word we use for work that is fatiguing and monotonous and a source of no particular pleasure. Many love the work they do, they love solving problems. They have no qualms about a long day. They don't concern themselves with their own potential. They are not ecstatic about the future, but that's fine. Most don't want wealth, power, control, although some do. Every single one wants a better life, an easier life.

## COMMON UNDERSTANDINGS: CORY

He says, "You know the old saying, 'The only thing worse than having a job is not having a job.'"

"Actually," I say, "I've never heard that."

I've led a sheltered life; I've always had a job. I've always had a shelter.

"Here's my version," he says. "It's easier to go to work than to survive as a bum."

# UNCOMPENSATED: ANTONIO

"I could have been paid by the VA to take care of my father, but I turned it down. My father's psychiatrist told me about this program and that I could be compensated for being home with him. It didn't seem right. He was my father. I didn't need any money. I had no income, but I had a pension."

# ON THE WATER: DENNIS

"The water is so clear, the quahogs are not coming back. I saw on the TV news this restaurant that I used to park my boat in front of—not too far out—and there were no boats there on the TV. Empty. There ain't a lot of clams no more, I hear."

"Did you get the Yamaha motor?" I ask.

He ignores me. "You know they put in that tunnel under the city that now stores rainwater and sewage. In the old days the city poured sewage onto the floor of the bay; the quahogs ate it and filtered it happily. Whatever that tunnel did, cleaning things up, the clams didn't like it."

He tells me this not to complain but only to set forth, so that I may understand, the sheer naked reality of his existence.

"Off Goddard Park used to be a gold mine. I'd work in the morning from 8:00 to 12:00 and make $500 to $800. Not enough clams anymore. My friend Owen who built his own boat, he's off the water now. Maybe it's his age. I'm a good digger, but he and his pals are better than me. They have more years in. They knew exactly where clams set up on the banks. GPS helps, but it's a trade, knowing the best spots to rake changes as the bottom changes. The old-timers have tricks. They don't tell you what they know; you have to learn it yourself."

The long barrel of his ribs moves in and out as he sighs.

"Here's my worst fear in life: What will I do if there are no clams anymore? But yeah, I got the motor."

# OFF THE BOOKS: RAYMOND

"When I'm out of work, all I do is worry about bills, and not providing for my family as men are supposed to."

He sees himself as losing value right before my eyes. I can tell it's hard for him to say.

"If I had a lot of money, I wouldn't work for a while. But I couldn't not work permanently. I'd feel lazy. Even if I had disability pay, I'd work off the books. I like having something to do."

# BLESSINGS: GINA

"God blessed me. I was out there for years and maybe four times had a knife pulled on me, and only once a gun. I managed to get decent men. Men never hurt me, although once I had Mace sprayed in my face and the undercover cops made me trade with them—sex for no arrest.

"Always in the car. I took them to one of the spots I knew. My friend said before I started it would be easy money, and I only had to work 9:00 PM to 2:00 AM. But a lot of them refused to pay me.

"Every night I was petrified. Every night I prayed to get home."

# WHAT YOU HAVE TO DO: SAL

"I was one of those people who made money without doing anything. Now *that* was a challenge, living by your wits. Seeing if I was smarter than the cops. Buy low, sell high. You just need capital to keep moving. I never ran out of capital.

"I got to Kennedy Plaza at 5:00 in the morning before the pawn stores opened, looking for people trying to get rid of gold jewelry and watches. I was home by 7:00 AM when my mother got up. That was the end of my work day. I crowded my work into those one and a half hours. You do what you have to do."

# CITY METAL: DEREK

"Copper wire arrives by the truckload, and we recycle it. Strip the rubber off the electrical wire in this machine. Make it come clean. I run the machine.

"In the old days, we would throw gas on the wire and burn it in a field to expose the copper. But it gave off this poisonous fume."

Thinking about those more dangerous days, his head falls back against the wall in relief.

"I get pretty dirty cleaning the machine. Worse, the wire is wrapped in asbestos, and I have to shake dust off by hand from the tubes. Even with a mask, it's hard to breathe."

Forty-four percent of the wealthy wake up three hours before work starts versus three percent of the poor.

# PRIVILEGED: DREW

"They treat the Spanish people the worst. Hire them as temps and pay them less. They don't get overtime, even after working forty-eight hours in a week or twelve hours in a day. They get no vacation. It's ridiculous. No health care. It's like two countries. The company is running a scam.

"They wouldn't put them on the payroll, and when they finally did, not one white person complained. We didn't have to feel guilty anymore."

I can tell he trusts the people who work under him and inspires their trust in return.

## PANDEMIC: JONATHAN

"It's not as secluded as I like. But I do my part to stay safe from the virus. I wipe everything down where anyone might have touched. Then someone gets infected, and they call me and say I *might* have been exposed, and I miss fourteen days of work, and lose two thousand bucks. 'Possibly exposed,' they tell me."

He pauses, like he's waiting for me to write a note so he can go back earlier, and if I can't, he at least wants me to be on his side, agreeing with the ridiculousness of the world.

# OLDER WORKERS: TIFFANY

"I wear short shorts and a tank top, like at Hooters. I work 11:30 AM to 5:00 PM, daytime hours so I can get my son. Most of the other girls are eighteen, and I'm almost forty. They want me to look good, and I don't look so great these days when I dance."

She sees me for anxiety, heart palpitations. The boy's father threatens to take her to court, claiming she's a lousy mother. Mostly, he promises to visit with the boy and doesn't show up.

"I'm tense. I have to pick up my son every day. I feel the constant judgement. The constant competition. I'd feel out of place even if I wasn't older.

"I knew what I was getting into. My father was sick and needed me to take care of him. You can't live on the salary of a substitute teacher, so I took the job."

## TAKE IT OR LEAVE IT: JAVON

"I can operate a forklift and weld. I have electric skills. I won't take on more responsibility though unless they pay me more. Everyone comes to get a paycheck first and foremost. Do I want to be a stronger employee with a broadened horizon? I'm not so sure."

He lifts his shoulders in a gesture of incomprehension.

# DO IT YOURSELF: REGGIE

"You work for two or three years at twelve-, thirteen-hour shifts, and you're going to tweak your neck, tear a rotator cuff. Everyone has surgery. The body is not meant to do what we do. Carrying 120 pounds up and down thirty steps. It's the heavy lifting and the lack of help, too many people standing around playing with their phones when others are working."

His chest is like a car radiator. His left arm looks as if it's been dipped in tattoos.

"You end up doing it yourself without waiting for them to stop sending pictures to their friends so that you can get home at a reasonable time to sleep to prepare for the next shift. But also, we're just short on help, or people are hurt or home with kids. Today I was frustrated and angry that others weren't helping, so I lifted the pile myself, and I heard my back crack like a knuckle. It probably won't hurt until tonight.

"But I still like the physical work because after the shift I feel good unless I hurt myself; I get some exercise, I breathe better.

"There are no background checks here. Who else would do this job except felons?"

Opioid overdose rates are highest among occupations with the greatest physical work demands and least access to paid sick leave.

# HAS TO BE: KEN

"I took the hose off the pump truck and took it around. Big fat hose. Very heavy. I dragged it all day shooting cement. It was about making money. I didn't love it, but I did it. It has to be about money if you're bent over all day. Mostly, I didn't want a job where I was up all night."

# UNDERSTANDING: RIGOBERTO

"The first day I drove the box truck to pick up supplies at the warehouse, I hit somebody. I'd driven a box truck before, but I owned a little car. I wasn't thinking: This is not a car, it's a truck. I rubbed against this guy's bumper while he was sitting in the car."

He takes off his glasses and rubs his eyes. His face, as he turns to me, has a clean startled look to it.

"I called the owner of the company to ask him the insurance information and apologize. He said, 'Shit happens.'"

## BEGINNINGS: DENNIS

"There's no one to help me." He sounds somewhere between frantic and defeated.

"The boat is in the water, but the motor is at the mechanic's twenty miles away.

"The guy at the marina wants me to get boat insurance." His voice climbs; he is outraged. "I never had boat insurance before. I used to keep it parked in my backyard when I lived by the water. So now I have to get insurance, which will mean a payment plan because I don't have any money right now.

"But mostly I need someone to help me get it out of the water onto a trailer and drive it to the mechanic's shop. There's no one to help. Bobbie is in rough shape on liver meds, and Caesar got his onto a trailer alone, so I haven't asked him."

Pride is getting in the way of his work, his only hope for income.

"Ask Caesar, he'll help you," I say, not knowing a thing about Caesar or whether he would or wouldn't, but eager for my patient to get to work.

"Yeah, I did get him started in the business," he says reflectively.

What I always like about seeing him, even when I am frustrated with his lack of progress, is that he does not try to pass himself off as anything other than what he is. There is no irony in his voice, no distance from himself, no awareness that people can assume different roles in his life.

# EXECUTION: SAM

"It's dangerous bringing power into a house from the street lines. Touch the wrong wires together or touch the metal siding when the wires touch, and I might be a dead man."

His hands are hairless, so I can see the scratches and burn marks clearly.

"But I'd do that street work rather than run wires under a porch in the mouse and dog shit. Even my boss acknowledges that that's nasty work. He throws me a few extra bucks for my positive attitude."

# FOOT SOLDIER: HENRY

"I have a Morton's neuroma. After fifty yards, my right foot goes dead. Pins and needles—feels like my sock is bunched up underneath, and I reach down to adjust it. I'm able to work through it. I'm stupid. I probably should have seen a doctor earlier."

# YOU NEVER KNOW: JAMES

"I work in textiles with Burmese people. Immigrants, people who are low on the totem pole. I have a soft spot for people who work their asses off, who want their kids to be better.

"There's this one older guy; he was around sixty. I said hello to him every day, and he always had a smile; everyone liked him. One day we hear he killed a cop. People ripped him apart, and the whole Burmese community part made it worse, but I had always thought he was gentle.

"Then we come to find out he was a CIA undercover over there, and he had flashbacks, and the day he shot the cop he had one—he snapped. I didn't understand what happened over there, what he must have gone through. You don't really know people, even when you work with them every day."

He tries to reason everything out, but it's hard to come to conclusions.

# NO REST: JAMIE

He has a fever and wants something for his cough. I tell him he'd look less ill if he combed his hair, and that gets him to smile.

"I'm threatened if I miss a shift. My boss will fire me. My mother depends on the money I send home. I'll work if I'm sick, until I fall. I'm twenty-five; what symptoms could be that serious?"

## SEATED: CORINNE

"I'll be a phlebotomist, I thought. They make good money—$20 an hour in the hospital, $35 if you go to people's houses like a visiting nurse. A friend of mine who's a nurse thinks I'd be good. I can stand the sight of blood; it don't bother me. I need to save $600 for the eight-week course."

Her legs are mummified in white gauze, yellowed by pus. Her shoes are slip-on sneakers.

"At my last cashier job my left leg still swelled when I was on my feet too much, after like three hours. But the lady who draws my blood gets to sit down between patients or when she's writing out labels."

# DIRECTIONS: VITO

"You lose a weekly paycheck and you lose vacation time, routine, relationships. When you have a job, your car just knows its way to work."

# OVERBOARD: DENNIS

"The last time I went out, a year ago, I wasn't in shape. My friend who took me said I smelled like booze. But he owed me because the year before he lost my anchor, the little one I lent him. He must have forgotten to tie the anchor well enough to the boat, and he covered ground slowly, and it probably just dropped off as he drifted. If I go back, I'll get a big anchor with a safety line and float so I don't lose track."

"*If* you go back?" I ask, either encouragingly or impatiently, depending on how he wants to hear it.

I assume he would want to provide an explanation, but he does not.

Five thousand workers die on the job annually, with injuries sustained by nearly three million more.

# 5

# STRUCTURE

The *Oxford English Dictionary* has thirty-nine definitions of work, stretching over pages of print I need a magnifying glass to read. "Something to be done, or something to do; what a person has or had to do; occupation, employment, business, task, function." "Action involving effort or exertion directed to a definite end, especially as a means of gaining one's livelihood; labor, toil." As a noun: "A particular act or piece of labor," "a thing made, a manufactured article or object." And as a verb: "to do, perform, practice (a deed, course of action, labor, task, business occupation, process)." When I've read through the thirty-nine, I find myself thinking about the saying "magic 'works,'" and that what we mean is that it achieves what it proposes, which is how I think of the purpose of a job. A job is what someone asks you to do. The jobs I hear about are remunerated, purposeful efforts that provide goods or services for another.

My patients work with their hands performing labor that must be physically comprehensible. The first thing I notice when I walk into the room is their hands, reaching out to shake mine, gripping their knees, fingers crossed on top of their chests as they lie back to catnap if I am running late. Wind and cold and violent exercise have worked over hands that are gray and cracked, pinky fingers splayed at odd angles, thumbs nicotine-tipped. At work, my patients are trying to do things that are not expressed in words, very often that are the direct opposite of words. Hands speak and sometimes reveal who they are.

Each morning for the past few months, starting at 7:15 AM, I hear the low hum of a generator switched on and then the rhythmic beat of hammers on wood. There is a new house going up behind mine. They started in November and worked in the bitter cold with balaclavas and hoodies. Each morning I could barely wait to get to the window at the back of my house to learn that day's task. I looked through the bare-branched tree between us and nervously watched as they walked up and down the steep slope of the roof, a nail-gun power cord in one hand, a harnessing rope in the other, somehow finding a way to attach plank to plank. They walked *across* ladders. Bravery seems concentrated in certain professions. I found myself absorbed by the progress, the poured concrete, the framing, the flooring. Insulation? Cut-outs for windows? To my seated eye, each hour, each day was an impressive display of competence. These are people who understand the word *man-made*, or better, *hand-made*.

Strength and physicality in work interest me, probably because it is so different from what I do as a primary care physician, although there are certainly doctors who work with their hands: surgeons and cardiologists implanting pacemakers, and radiologists threading tubes into arteries. I steered clear of this kind of medical practice. My kind of work requires a lighter concentration that allows me to be dreamy and perhaps more attentive to what patients say.

I do not want to be sentimental. Not everyone can "get ahead" working where they work. Much of any job is drudgery, monotony. Manual labor is often dirty, exhausting, tedious, unpleasant. There are good reasons to avoid it. Dissatisfied and miserable at work, people are sometimes violent at home. I do not want to promote the false belief that anyone can succeed, or that everyone will at some point derive deep satisfaction from their employment. It is of course a fantasy that thrift and hard work will be enough to secure the American dream. We know better. This is not a book about the wrongs of the modern world, despairing the brute indignities of manual labor that reduces women and men to cogs. Nor is *A Living* an elegy for work. Rather, it is about how people find work respectable, or don't. Work is a structure that helps people figure out what they need, security or freedom.

## COVERED: DAWN

"I worked for a ninety-two-year-old. I had a friend who knew she needed an aide. I liked working without anyone breathing down my neck. I'd leave a report for her son, who lived with her, at the end of the day.

"I did more cleaning of the house than anything else. She didn't really talk because she had dementia. I dressed her, gave her meals, gave her her meds. She used to shit herself. Her bed was covered with it, her commode was covered, and she was too. Her commode was in the room, but she didn't make it there. She thought it was funny; she laughed like she was a kid.

"I did it for extra money—it paid the bills. If I didn't have that money, like when she went into a nursing home, I had to adjust."

# SECURITY: EASTMAN

"I got a uniform, an earpiece, an ID badge. I took the job after this bullshit certification class. Two hours. What you can and can't do. No kind of training. I know the people who own the security company. They hired me because I know how to fight.

"I frisk people, make sure they don't have drugs on them or weapons, make sure people pay their bills. But I don't have power really. I'm basically a civilian with the responsibility to come over and help. I have an inviting face. I deal well with the wealthier crowd. I don't curse.

"The worst are the ones who just turned old enough to drink. They come at me. 'Why are you a security guard?' they ask when I let them in. 'Enjoy the night and go home safe,' I say.

"I get called the other night at this party we're covering, and from a distance I see it's a guy I know, a big guy, and he's agitated. He sees me and he relaxes. He's very drunk.

"I say, 'I can't let you back into the main room, you know, unless you forgot something inside, and then I can walk you in and out.' He doesn't need to go in, and I say, 'You better get going before the cops get here. The team up here has already called.' He thanked me and left with a few girls.

"The next morning, I hear he died in a car crash on the highway that night, driving drunk."

# BEAT: OWEN

"I work in a big garage with machinery—but it's open, like a gazebo—recycling glass, cardboard, plastics. Physically, I can't do winters. Once it goes below fifteen degrees, I can't beat it. I work twelve hours a day, but the young guys go fourteen for the extra money."

# MEMORIES: DENNIS

"I pumped the boat yesterday. Got the water from the hull. There's this plate, the size of a sewer cap, and if it's not locked down right—water. I didn't keep it super tight because in the winter it seizes up. And I spent $200 for a $600 lid.

"Now I have to pay this guy to power wash the bottom to get the scum off so it's smooth as a surfboard. Right now there's growth on the bottom.

"There used to be eighty of us out there in the water in a small area. A big party. Yelling at this guy for scratching my boat, and that guy for having too loud an engine. I'd go out where other boats were so I could holler out if I needed help."

He is going over it again, the best memories from not so long ago. He had put on weight—the muscles no longer showed through his skin—but now he's losing it again, coming out of hibernation, his waist thinning. And he's getting hopeful again. As am I.

"But the other guys don't have my spots. If I ever get back to my spots, the clams may still be there."

## CONFUSIONS: LISA

"I worked as a waitress at a breakfast place. I was up at 4:00 AM opening the place, and by 6:00 I was miserable. I couldn't figure out why everyone was so happy in the morning."

## LOOKING TO HELP: TIANA

"Best job I ever had was at an Alzheimer's house. There was this woman who waited out in the hall for the next girl's shift to start. Every night she didn't know me. Every night I'd come in, and she'd introduce herself to me. 'Oh, you're the new girl. How are you?'

"I liked working overnight because I don't sleep anyway. If I'm up, I'd rather be working. Alzheimer's patients are up at night folding things or taking imaginary field trips.

"In the morning before I left, I made breakfast or did laundry, and this same lady was always standing behind me, looking to help."

# ENAMELLING: MARA

"I liked to get up and feel like part of the working population. Rushing out to catch a bus. At the factory, I sat in a row of eight girls, four on either side of the table in a hot room with the oven in the corner. When the jewelry went into the oven and came out cool, it was handed over to us.

"I had syringes with colored paint which I controlled with a foot pedal. My quota was three hundred earrings a day. I'd put a line of yellow next to a line of red, into the grooves in the metal. Sometimes blue and red. We listened to country music."

She is not carefree or lighthearted, but maybe she was a little bit more back then.

# PLUMBER: TODD

"A sewer backup is the worst. You got a very stressed customer. If we don't clear the line, your yard will get dug up. We can ruin the basement though, break a pipe, or break the snaking machine, which is expensive. We're running blind, trying to get roots out of the pipe. We don't know where to run the snake. A lot can go wrong. I get stressed just talking about it."

## SHOW-OFF: WARREN

He rolls his shoulders forward and backward with a calm grimace.

"I was a steeplejack. No one knew how to do it, that's what I liked. I was like a circus performer. I was a show-off. I knew tricks. People would come out at lunch to watch me swing around the smokestacks I was painting. I felt proud. I made good money. I could cut out early and go home. Get paid for ten hours and work four."

## RE-CALL: ROBBIE

"I get ice. I check the liquor stock. I cut fruit—limes, lemons." He talks slowly, wincing from time to time, although he's never announced that he has pain. Maybe it's just puckering, thinking of the citrus.

"A bunch of young kids work with me. Servers. Friday night one of them left the outside door open, and so many bugs got in, it was insane. We all needed flyswatters. At the end of the night my boss told me I sucked as a bartender. I wasn't good at the side work, he said, the roll-ups, where you put the utensils in the napkins. He said I give him an attitude."

He clicks his tongue in disgust, turns away. I could see why a boss might find him a little lethargic and unapologetic, might miss his dark humor.

"He didn't put me on Saturday. I asked him why not, I've worked here for fourteen years. 'Because I need you to be a better bartender,' he said.

"On Saturday, fifty people come in, and he realizes not many people can handle that rush. But I can. He calls me back on Sunday. I do it my way, make the people happy, get it done."

# REVENGE: KIERSTEN

"My favorite patient is the one who wants me fired. Says I'm no good as a nursing aide. Pretends like she's angry. After every doctor visit she goes in and sits with my manager and complains to her about me. But I know it's all a performance. She'd miss complaining about me.

"I enjoyed the day her son and grandson hid her car. She was talking to my manager, and they came in and said they couldn't find the car they'd driven to the appointment. She and they all went out to the parking lot and couldn't find it. She came back in and told my manager someone stole her car from *our* lot, and asked what kind of place was this? I liked seeing her face when her son and grandson came in behind her and told her the truth."

# ROUGH WATER: KARL

"Before we leave, I'm responsible for filling the tanks with fresh water, enough for two weeks out, and for food shopping—a lot of milk and ice cream. I buy myself Ensure, in case I don't have time to eat, and frozen cheeseburger sliders that I can microwave.

"We usually leave the dock around 10:00 AM and ride for twenty-four or thirty-six hours into the middle of the ocean. We set up the nets and the tables to pack the fish on. Two nets on hydraulic drums off the back of the boat. It takes about ten minutes for nets to go down, and then we hook the tops onto heavy doors on the sides of the boat to spread them. The captain can tell how full they are; there are sensors on them when they expand. Sometimes it takes twenty minutes to fill the nets, sometimes three hours. We monitor the ropes, check the cans, the buoys.

"When it's a full bag, we haul them up, open them on the deck, and fish pour out, sometimes as high as our stomachs. Squid: Illex in the summer, Loligo in the winter. Or mackerel, herring, and butterfish depending on what we're after. We push them through open doors in the mid-deck floor to the tanks in the processing room. Then a conveyor runs them up onto the table, and we go down there and put them into boxes in winter, plastic bags in summer, twenty-five pounds apiece, and then into the freezer.

"We don't sleep much. The crew's twelve rough guys who can take a joke; if you can't, you're not invited back. Twenty-four hours at home and then back out for another two weeks."

## KNEELING: VINCENT

He grimaces as he sits down, his joints protesting.

"I used to tile and bust my balls to make a living. I walked on my knees across entire buildings."

# COMPLAINTS: VICTORIA

"I would think people would help each other, but no. I can't trust anyone.

"My boss asks me, 'Are you eating at your station?'

"'Yes,' I say. I know the rule about bringing food into the machine room.

"'Someone complained.'

"'Denise, right?' I ask. He doesn't answer. 'Unbelievable,' I say."

He makes a scowl like this hurts more than the kidney stone he recently passed.

"Why didn't Denise say anything to me? I would never email the boss."

# EASIER: ROBERT

"I quit school at fifteen and started doing walls. Carrying a big mortar bed about the size of your exam table that you mix cement in. Sixty shovels of sand; two bags, ninety pounds each, of cement; two bags clay; one bag perlite. Mix it with a hoe. Lots of effort. I was a skinny kid with big muscles. No one helped me clean up. It took too much time; it was too hard."

He nods and swallows loudly. I stare at the scallop shells of his deltoid muscles.

"Between the studs you put in a wire sheet and add a cement layer to the panels of the lattice, and you'd scrape it up to make a wall. You had to plumb the wall, make it the right depth, one inch thick.

"It had to be done by noon so the tile guys could come in the afternoon. My boss was always yelling at me. I was afraid to lift my arm the wrong way."

He moves his thick hands like a mime. His eyes drop. He smiles uncertainly.

"Now it's easier: you nail cement or gypsum board up and paint it. We didn't know any better back then; it was all I knew at the time."

# SURF AND TURF: DENNIS

"How did I know I was okay again? This guy came to my spot, and I hollered, 'What are you, lost?'

"If I find clams and you're not my friend, I don't want you to be around. Quahoggers fall into two groups—jealous people and friendly people."

# BOUNCER: BYRON

"I'm a little guy; I need to keep the big guys away from me. I bought my own handcuffs and baton, even though they're illegal to carry. But I can talk people down. I'm good at that. It's shitty pay, no extra on weekends, not really any overtime. But I get to be around music all night. I love it."

He is slight—bright eyes, thin bones.

"I get called to deal with the crazy dudes, the loud ones. The other night this guy, he got drunk and stood in front of the swinging door to the kitchen, and I had to ask him to move. 'I'll do whatever the fuck I want,' the one last night says. There are cameras on, and one of the first rules is never to touch them until they touch you. Or unless he threatens you. I keep my hands up in the air to show him I don't want trouble. But after the third time that I ask him to move and he doesn't, I push him toward the door.

"Outside, he swings at me and I duck, and I hit him only once. Then I realize he is too drunk to fight back, even though he's going to try, and I tell the valet to call the cops.

"Meanwhile I tell the kid to get going or he's really going to get in trouble. The cops come, and he keeps mouthing off at them until they put him in the car and take him to jail."

## DRESSED FOR SUCCESS: RUSSELL

"At the foundry we made parts for cars. I pushed the core carrier, which was best for me because I didn't like to work in the heat. We made black sand molds. I was trained in molds. I put the mold in the shakers, which would knock the sand off the metal."

There is not a scrap of fat on him. His white shirt is pulled taut by his chest.

"This one guy poured iron in a tuxedo; he came to work in a tuxedo. That made me laugh."

# HARDENING: DUANE

"I do cement. Walkways, garages, basements, stairs, around pools. It's about marking and leveling, which I check with a line or laser and my good eye. I build a form out of wood, and the cement truck arrives and puts its chute down (you buy by the yard). With all the chemicals in it, it doesn't set right away. So you pull on rubber boots and walk through it with a rake called a come-along. Pull and push and pat, but mostly it levels itself if it's the right wetness. There's a guy at the other end standing on a two-by-four like a surfboard, dipping it up and down; that helps level it too, and takes out bubbles."

None of his life makes me envious; it is rough work, grubby.

"Then the finishing part using trowels to smooth things—my favorite. You lay out two wide boards that don't sink while it's still wet. You stand on one, and you bend and smooth and then step backward onto the next board and pick up the one you were standing on. I can't stand the waiting for two or three hours."

He has a restless, angular energy; it's hard to imagine him waiting two or three minutes.

"As you know, I have OCD, which is good for cement work. I have to make stuff that looks good. I have to be proud of the work. Everyone I work with says I'm a good worker because I never put my hands in my pockets or take a phone call. I'm always ready and waiting. I talk a little too much. But it's hard to find good help, so most people put up with that. The muscle soreness the next day—that feels good."

"Sounds like you're damn good at it," I say. He wants my approval, and when I give it, he tucks his hands into his armpits.

# DIRT: CHESTER

"I had to work on the tumbler today because one of the guys was out. The tumbler gives cement an aged look for landscape work and retaining walls and stone driveways. You put in grit, sand, cement, pigment, admix and pour into a mold. A tamper puts down thirty thousand pounds of pressure and vibrates. It comes onto a plate and then onto a conveyor."

He usually schedules visits at the end of his day, on his way home. His heavy canvas pants are filmed with dust. He moves slowly, carefully, as if he's still on the job. He's told me about coworkers losing fingers.

"A cement factory is a dirty industry. You can't get away from the dust. Even with dust masks you can't get away."

His thick hair is powdered white, and I imagine him as an older man. From the looks of it, he will never go bald.

"They say ten years of silica puts you at risk of silicosis, and I'm getting there."

# OLD DAYS: DENNIS

He is back on the water, and his hands are smooth and tan as if a dog had licked coarse brown salt from them all day. The sun has tightened his face.

"My friends are mad at me. They want to see the old me. Rip out in the morning, work, go in—like the old days. They say, 'Shit, where you been?'

"I'm a little scared. My mother, who's always negative, said to me, 'Give that job up.' And maybe she's right.

"I have to hang on to thirty feet of pipe, draw a rake across the ocean bottom, and pull it in. I use a short rake and start on the side of the boat. I hang over the side and rake; my arms never stop. There's another technique. Many clammers use a long rake, start on one side of the boat, and walk it back. It's been a while, and I know I'm not in shape. Yes, I can use a winch sometimes to help me pull, but I need a battery for my winch, and I still can't afford that.

"I'm sleeping better," he says, trying to give me credit for something, to share in his success.

The medicine I'd given him for his broken sleep has helped him fall asleep but probably added only fifteen minutes of rest to any given night. Mostly, he's drinking less now that he's saving for a new battery.

Health insurance accounts for nearly 40 percent of the cost of hiring a low-wage worker.

# MUSIC: HEATHER

"I worked at Roller Kingdom for eight years. First, making pizza in the snack bar, then renting out skates, then as a skating guard, blowing a whistle at the teenagers skating backward during the all-skate hour when the beginners were on the floor. I would have to kick them off for twenty minutes if they didn't listen. The parents would come up to me and scream at me for reprimanding their child."

She's having fun remembering, laughing out loud, quite pleased with herself.

"Then I became a DJ there. I was from a musical family. My father played in a band, and my sister is a music teacher, and my other sister sings a cappella, and I loved DJing for the skaters. We used records; the manager would go out a buy a new stack every week. Two turntables. Matinees, I'd do Top 40. Saturday nights, dance music, hip-hop. Fridays, heavy metal. We had open requests, and kids would come up to the window.

"I loved skating between sets. I had custom speed skates, bright yellow with pink wheels and laces, and chrome bearings. In all my years, we had no overdoses, no one got beat up, no one got shot. Empty nip bottles in the bathroom, that was about the worst. When I became manager, when I had to handle money, it became a job."

# ICING: GREG

"People skate all day and all night at a public rink. If a group was on for an hour, we cleaned the ice with the Zamboni. After an hour it got pretty gouged. We used blades to smooth it, the augurs to suck up the snow, and then we'd brush the snow out of the corners. If we went too fast around the corners, we'd wipe out. Think of a car with studs in the tires. By the end of the night, you're cold."

I don't skate. I don't like the cold. I dread winter, yet despite my complaining, I've never moved south, away from it. I think of Zambonis as armadillos, prehistoric creatures.

"The best part was taking the little kids out for a ride and doing donuts on the ice. And looking down their moms' shirts when they came to fetch their kids down."

# BARRELS: MAURICE

"I did garbage for the city. I retired after thirty years with 80 percent of my pay. I wanted to be a fireman but never got hired."

I know he plays golf three times a week—he wears golf shirts to his visits—so this recent work history is unexpected.

"Garbage is kind of the worst job in the world. You'd never believe the shit we found. A coin collection of silver dollars—I still have it. Copper and brass that we sold by the pound. New clothes. The worst smell was dead grass that had been sitting in a barrel too long. Also, dog shit and maggots.

"We were only two guys working 7:00 AM to 11:00 AM. No breaks. But sometimes you got to go home early; that was the incentive, you go home when you're finished.

"I wasn't embarrassed by it; I made good money. Right to the shower when I got home. A bad day was when the truck broke down and you had to wait for it to get fixed, and then you'd go back out for your pick-ups and the day went ten hours. That was a bad day."

He shakes his head, remembering. The freckles spread out on the back of his hands from years of sun.

"The highway department and sanitation department butted heads. If one of our guys was out, one of their guys had to work the garbage truck. Some of their guys went along but refused to work. They'd sit and watch. That led to some good fistfights."

# SURVEILLANCE: CRAIG

"I'm watched all the time, and there are rules. With GPS now they know where you are. We carry dash cams. If you get into an accident, they've recorded eight seconds before and four after." He speaks in a conspiratorial tone.

"All right," I say.

"There is no tolerance for drugs or alcohol, no cigarettes either. I have no problem with that. I never had an accident, knock wood. What I don't like is that they can hear your conversation. I don't mind that they can watch me. The audio is the problem. You know, the truck is my home. If I'm talking to my doctor, or my girlfriend, they could be listening anytime."

I like how he mentions his doctor to draw me onto his side.

# SAFETY: ROY

"I started in plumbing with small companies, but now I'm with a giant, eight-state company. In the old days if I cut my hand or hit my head, I'd go and get stitched up and get back to work. Now I get written up. There's a corrective action. 'Every accident is preventable' is their mantra, but that's not reality."

He looks disconsolate, perplexed.

"Each morning, I get a daily schedule and a set of criteria for safety. I have to wear safety glasses all the time on the job; if I take them off, I've broken the rule and can get reported. They talk a good game about safety, but they don't back you up. They've taken it to a level of silliness but think nothing of having you work a sixteen-hour shift."

## NONSTOP: SHARLENE

"I work in the preschool with twenty kids, ages three to five. I'm always running around. At 8:30 the kids get dropped off. Each parent has to be let in individually, so I'm running to the door and watching the kids over my shoulder. I try to keep the kids who are already there in their activities. I store the lunches. Then the phone calls start—paper product salesmen, software salesmen, advertising agencies. Parents who call and want five minutes to talk even though they were just there and can hear in the background how busy it is.

"I get up and down from the floor with the kids, each one doing their own thing. Then we do snacks. Then we do exercise time like hokey pokey or yoga, or we have a parade. From 12:00 to 2:00 they are supposed to stay on their mats, but they don't all sleep, and some of them can't stay on their bed. There's not a day that goes by without someone having an accident in their pants.

"It's better for me mentally to work full time. When I get home, though, there are things I'd like to do, but I'm too tired."

Work has switched our spending patterns from tangible goods—clothes, cars, furniture—to services such as childcare, health care, and fast food. In 1950, spending on services accounted for 40 percent of GDP; today the proportion is more than 70 percent.

# HAIR: DAVID

"The key is not to panic. You get in there, and you can get lost. You can't follow the lines. Hair is weight. You can shift weight. You don't know that at first. It took me ten years to learn it. Weight changes the shape of the face."

For a moment, I wish that I had hair again. As it was thinning and disappearing—before I started to buzz off what was left myself—I dreaded going to the barber, looking in the mirror, watching how little hair fell to the floor.

"You can't just shift the hair alone, you have to put it somewhere. So you distribute it to make an oval, to centralize the looker's eyes on the eyes and cheekbones. You're building. You need good pressure, and you have to lay your hands in all different positions. You cut flat against the skull to get a baseline. You cut along the fingers, and the fingers have to be flat against the skin. But that's only the perimeter.

"Then you put in a little mistake, which is the technique of taking a straight line into a soft line. For it to look natural, you need mistakes—a little rough, a tiny bit uneven."

# HOW TO MANAGE: MICKEY

"I manage buildings. No one bothers me. No one is behind me. I'm the best cleaning guy—greasy stoves, showers. I use oven cleaner on tub stains, that's my secret. I take apart the stove and soak it down, which usually takes two days."

His old man's neck skin has hieroglyphic patterns of wrinkles. Cracked clay.

"I do vacancy preps, before the next person moves in. I put compound in cracks in the walls and sand them, then two coats of paint. Anyone who tells you one coat is enough is lying; no paint I've ever found does one coat."

I want to hire him to fix up my house. But of course, I can't cross that line, involve him in my home life. I'd hire almost any of my patients if I could.

"I listen to talk radio. If my boss ever checks in, he has to say something of course. He says, 'Get that door fixed.' I know about the door. I'm already on it."

His hand is a hinge, its own piece of machinery.

"When I'm home, I never just sit and watch TV. I have no patience. I've never watched a whole movie. On vacation, I work. I did my buddy's cellar—repainting, redoing the stucco the other day.

"I like managing buildings, though, because I live there too—free rent, no electric or gas bill, none of that. Money stays in my pocket."

## MEALS: TERRI

"I'm thankful I have hours. Even when the chef is angry and makes me wait for orders, or when the boss yells at me, 'You need to clean that table faster.' I know she's a witch, but I can't argue with her. She has a problem keeping her mouth shut.

"I like my job: I smile. I take care of them. I please them. Whatever they want I get them. I'm paid $3.89 an hour, so I need my tips. People take care of me. I feel appreciated. I give the same care to everyone, whether they tipped the last time or not. I love just being able to be me, and I make money doing it. I don't like the people who come in and are miserable, but I still say, 'My name is T. What can I get you to drink?' Before I finish, the miserable ones say, 'Coffee two eggs over. Home fries.'"

I can see it matters very much to her, making them all happy.

"I don't like working with teenagers; there's always drama. They are always on the phone; I can't stand it. They stop working when the phone rings, right in the middle of customers. They pick up the phone—who does that?

"At home, I get depressed; I can't stand it. At home I fight with my mother, who complains about my daughter and expects me to cook her dinner. I say, 'Why don't you cook for me?'"

# RECYCLE: DEVON

"I work in the recycling part, not at the dump site itself. The trucks come into this giant warehouse building, open on one end, and dump the garbage on the floor—cardboard, milk containers, glass, paper. Then the bulldozers push it into a hopper, which sends it all out on a conveyor belt.

"There are three of us on each side of the belt pulling out things that don't belong—garden hoses, hangers, cloth, deer carcasses, sharps, weapons. When I worked on that line—it's all Spanish people working there now—I pulled out a frozen python snake. We leave the plastic and cardboard and glass. The conveyor runs into this machine that has a vision system and separates glass, aluminum, plastic, polypropylene (like coffee cups), milk jugs, cans, laundry detergent bottles, metal, soda cans, newspaper, cardboard. And these each go off into huge storage containers that have machinery to press them into bales, wrapped by wire.

"Now that I'm a manager, I do a lot of walking—twenty-five yards from the first machine to the last, about a hundred times a day. I walk a mile every hour. It's loud in there, and dusty, but it doesn't smell bad like over at the dump. No one makes less than $15 an hour, and there's medical."

## DRIVEN CRAZY: BRYAN

"People can't drive. They slam on the brakes. They cut me off. I don't understand it. They love to pull in front of me, always from my right. I'm driving a twenty-six-foot truck. The truck attracts crazies. If they're going to hit me, they'll hit me; I can't stop them. I lean on the horn. People don't care. But I'd rather be out driving than stuck inside the shop. I haven't had any accidents."

# DANCING: CIERRA

"I went in one afternoon and it was empty and the manager was at the bar and he looked at me and he signed me up for my first shift. The girl he had me shadow turned into my best friend. To work there you had to tip the DJ, the manager, and the scheduler. You had to show up with money in case you didn't make enough to pay those three.

"The first rule the afternoon girls taught me was *Don't get drunk.* I worked only afternoons. The nights are too sexual and there's too much hustling. I'd rather make friends with people. I could stand out during the day when I was twenty-one; there was less competition, not the cream of the crop, but the older, uglier. 'Rode hard and put away wet,' we used to say about them.

"Another rule was *By the third song, take off all your clothes.* You dance on stage and you get asked into a private room, so the job was less about dancing than dealing with people. I liked and knew about sports, so I always had something to talk about. You didn't drink because it's important that you remember things about the customers so they'd come back."

Although she speaks confidently, unsentimentally, I can tell she isn't sure of what she deserved back then, or today, or what I think of her.

"I never worried about getting hit. It could be bad for some girls at some places—some had pimps; some worked even when they were eight months pregnant. Women weren't allowed to walk in alone because some of them were looking for husbands or boyfriends, and they would get into fights with the girls or their men, and it was hard for security staff to handle.

"I knew my friends wouldn't walk in; they were in college and didn't have money to go to a club. I could leave with $300 most days. Three days a week, twelve to seven. Still, it was expensive; you had to have a different outfit each time you came out on stage.

"Good Friday was the most packed day—I'd write that one in my calendar every year. Weird, right? I don't know why—you get to eat meat that day or something?

"I stayed ten years. I paid for my son's pre-K. I had to stay in shape, but shaving my legs all the time was the most annoying, followed by the amount of makeup I used, but even that wasn't so bad. At a certain point you don't do it no more because you don't have to."

# WRONG NUMBER: ANDRE

"There are ten of us, each at an empty desk with a phone and a computer. I work 4:00 PM to 9:00 PM. I took the job because a friend of mine did it, and I couldn't find something better. I liked it because I could pace, turn the evening into my workout.

"I'd break the ice using my script. 'Congratulations, you are preapproved for a HomeSafe and Life Alert. We will put four cameras in your house and...' Most people just hang up, or they say, 'I have one,' or 'I'm interested, I know someone who has one,' or they flip out and say, 'I'm having dinner.'

"If someone is interested, I take the address, and the reps call them back to finalize. Every call felt like I was doing something wrong. If you push someone who is saying 'No' to you, it feels wrong. I suppose the system helped some people, but I was that person who annoyed you."

He's not a fast talker for a salesman. With me, he is in no hurry. He has all the time in the world.

"One week no one picks up and it seems pointless, and the next week everyone wants a Life Alert. I'm paid only on commission, about $200 a sale, but the money is pulled if no one is home when they go to install. The people I'm calling and the installation is in another state, so I never know if there really was no installation; maybe the sale never went through, or maybe the wife didn't want it. Or maybe the company just didn't want to pay me. I couldn't trust what the owner said."

## APPLES: CALEB

"There is something great about getting up early, before other people are up. We start every other Friday morning at 4:30 AM in the press room. We'd collected the fallen apples in the days before, and they sit in wooden, slatted bins around the room. We tip the bins toward the conveyor belt, and the apples line up and go forward, and we pick out the lousy ones. The grinder makes them into pomace. Under the presser, we make a tower of metal frames—a metal grid on the bottom, a stretch of cheesecloth, a layer of pomace, a thin sheet of plastic, then another metal grid, cheesecloth, pomace, plastic. The press makes it into cider, which drips into a holding container. Clear tubes take the juice into a UV filter area and then into quart and gallon jugs, and finally into the storage cooler. It's always a long day, but a relaxing day compared to planting trees or picking up brush. The room smells like Halloween."

## DONATIONS: DOUG

"I worked at Savers in shipping and receiving, and people would bring in random stuff. Or we had those big metal donation boxes you see on the street emptied and brought to us. Or when someone died or got evicted or whatever, these cleaning crews would go in, grab everything, and bring it to us."

He has a naïve, enthusiastic immediacy. He finds pleasure in most things. He is a young man moving forward in his life.

"We had three piles: clothing, toys, and jewelry, which also included coins that came out of people's pockets. Nine of ten times you'd find a jewelry box, sometimes even gold and diamonds which the cleaners hadn't seen. I had first pick of the clothes. I remember once finding a pistol and waving it in the air saying, 'What do I do with this?' Old records we didn't sell at the store, and I was into music, so I'd set it aside rather than throw them out. I found a nerve stimulation machine, an original Nintendo from the 1980s (the manager took that one to his office, and then it disappeared), keyboards, turntables.

"That job made me want to drive trucks, because I talked to the guys who brought stuff in, and they got paid better and got to move around more."

# HOME TEAM: CLEA

"Strip the bed, make the bed, dust, put out new glasses, towels, chocolate on the pillow. I have twenty minutes a room."

Her bitter tone suggests she is only stating the truth about a reality from which she has no chance of escape and that nothing can change.

"When the football players come to town, they leave the rooms terrible. Girls have been there with them; you can see the traces of blood in the sheets. I need a special bag for the empty bottles. The worst is the tub, trying to get out every hair."

# EXTERMINATOR: NATE

"It's about solving problems. There's an opossum on the roof, a bat in the house, a squirrel in the attic, cockroaches under the sink, a bees' nest by the porch. I get stung about twice a year. I set traps and put down poison, dangerous chemicals. Pest control is like a puzzle. I've learned to think like a rat."

One minute he is deadpan, the next his mouth is open with delighted laughter.

"People are either ashamed or afraid. I spend a lot of time calming people. Then I come back and pick up dead animals.

"I never know where I'll be the next day, but people always say thank you."

# MEDICINE: DENNIS

"You never do a telehealth visit instead of coming in," I say into the speakerphone on my desk. "Where are you?"

"I finally got on the boat. Being on the boat is the best medicine, doc. I feel like a fisherman."

"You *are* a fisherman," I say. "You mean you are calling me from your boat, and the boat's in the water?" I am a little incredulous.

"I'm rusty, but yeah, I'm hanging forty feet of pipe off the side as we speak. I'm trying to get in shape."

"How's that going?"

"My arms are not in shape. I've been sitting on my ass for a year. This feels like I'm at a gym or something."

"I'm proud of you," I say, and I am.

He laughs, rejecting the praise. "I needed to work. I was out of money. But look at this, there's a scuba diver ten yards from here, creeping around, trying to get my clams. In the old days I used to pineapple M-80s on the divers."

"Don't do that," I say, laughing.

"Sunglasses on, radio on, cruising across the water. That's me now, doc. I gotta go. Let me get back to work."

# ENDNOTE

# TIRED

Because my office can be a refuge, my patients express their tiredness. They don't so much sit as flop down in the chair. Not infrequently I've stepped out of the room to take a call, and when I return, they are snoring. For my patients, tiredness strikes with the force of sickness, and it is sometimes difficult for me to separate the two when evaluating them. Fatigue can be part of an illness, of course—think of depression or heart failure. Fatigue can feel like an injury. Dennis came in tired, without much sleep. He had the sleeplessness of chronic alcohol use. Maybe they sense that I am tired too. I like to think that my tiredness comes from being accessible to patients at times of trouble or exceptional circumstances. But maybe they can also feel my fatigue from carrying around all my small life and medical mistakes and guilt. There is also always, in a medical visit, the fatigue of looming catastrophe.

I see many varieties of tiredness. My image of tiredness comes from farmworkers up before sunrise who go to bed at sunset, and from manual laborers working in the sun or factory heat. (A doctor after a night on call is another image.) I recognize some of their fatigue. I know the exhaustion of the night shift. Eyelid-swollen lethargy. I remember my sons as infants, unable to sleep for more than forty minutes at a stretch. There is being tired from working in artificial light. There is the clumsiness of stepping back out into the morning street after a night awake. But I don't know the tiredness of the wheelbarrow or of pushing barrels up ramps or of hauling fish onto tables. I don't know the sensation of eight hours spent near great loud machines that can kill. Or eight hours of the cruel drudgery of cleaning toilets. Tired they are hungry; hungry, they are tired. Enervation from their lifelong exertions makes them seem older than they are.

Tiredness comes as a blast, as an inability to catch one's breath or to think things over clearly. Or it arrives as slowly as a change of weather, a barometric change. Fatigue distorts what my patients hear or see; it throws them off balance; it makes them less patient, more disenchanted; it highlights futility; its unendingness frightens them; it makes them ready for violence; they "fight off" tiredness. Theirs is too often the tiredness of feeling you have no other way out, when fatigue dominates your view of the world until all activity seems pointless.

Weariness empties the head. On the brink of collapse, sometimes they are too tired to speak. If they speak, they are too tired to raise their voices. But there can also be a tranquility in weariness, a quiet easygoingness. Fatigue makes them want to be alone, to be solitary; it excludes them from society. Their visit with me delays their arrival at home and time to nap. I am their last stop before bed. Sometimes they can be so tired that an escape into sleep is impossible.

Tiredness is omnipresent among my patients' problems. Although I have no easy medication for my patients' fatigue, if I acknowledge their look of tiredness—sympathy as understanding—I accept it, and that's enough perhaps, a moment of peace. They have earned their rest.

# CODA

Fifty years ago, when Studs Terkel published *Working*, he found that his interviewees were people in "search for daily meaning as well as daily bread, for recognition as well as cash, for astonishment rather than torpor; in short, for a sort of life rather than a Monday through Friday sort of dying." In these years following the twenty-first century's first pandemic, key labor-movement achievements still alive in Terkel's day—eight-hour days, with health care and pension—have unraveled.

We have some idea why blue-collar wages have stagnated in these last fifty years: a macroeconomic shift greatly raised the value of a college degree, owing in part to the decimation of manual labor by automation and globalization. Waves of deindustrialization devastated the lives of working-class Blacks, particularly after the Second World War. American manufacturing, always a male-skewing sector, contracted as a result of increased international trade.

A college-for-all narrative was emphasized as *the* pathway to success and stability. Patients of mine who don't own a family business still worry about the future of their children who don't choose this path. They don't want their kids "working with their hands." But as traditional college enrollment rates have risen nearly 30 percent this century, trade school enrollment has risen at twice this rate. Vocational and technical education costs far less than a traditional four-year degree, and a student can often learn a trade and enter a related profession in eighteen to twenty-four months, compared to the four years or longer it takes to earn a bachelor's degree. As I write, the manufacturing, infrastructure, and transportation fields are all expected to grow in the coming years—and many of those jobs likely won't require a four-year degree. Yes, many college *graduates* make more money—but less than half of students finish the degrees they start. This number drops as low as 10 percent for students in poverty.

In this new world after COVID-19, I want my patients to instruct me in what they do; not in an idealized way, but by explaining what their work consists of and their feelings about it. If a doctor asks his patients what they do all day in detail, they come to believe, perhaps, that what they do is important. Who else asks? Not their coworkers, or siblings or friends or partners. Describing their bodies on a good day, equilibrates, a bit, the powerless sensation patients feel at every doctor visit. At the same time, I can learn about them. Freud believed that along with love, work is one of "the cornerstones of our humanness."

People who enjoy their job report greater overall satisfaction with their lives. The causal influence of job satisfaction on life satisfaction remains under debate but reflects the importance of work in people's lives. Of course, job satisfaction, as I've seen with my patients, is moderated by age, self-employment, control of one's schedule, the importance of work among one's friends and family, the inner drive for achievement.

Two centuries ago, we were a country of farmers, and the ubiquity of physical work made us more egalitarian. No one retired; life expectancy was forty years. We have radically changed how we think of common work, essential work. What do you do? Who do you work for and where? What do you earn? The answers still define who you are and what you are contributing. The "work ethic" remains revered and preferable to unemployment. My patients care if work is reliable, remunerative, rewarding. Physical work has a bonus: it sometimes offers the particular allure of mastering in making, of a set of standards (shoes, driveways, clamming), of perfectibility. But after age sixty-five, manual labor is challenging. For a nation with national retirement benefits that is trying to keep up financially with an aging population, there are equity concerns about the retirement needs of those who worked physically difficult jobs.

Those of us without physical jobs have ceased to practice some important skills. Watching the roofers through my back window, I believe we have become more helpless. We now rely on automation and artificial intelligence, making us increasingly dependent on things over which we have little control. Surrounded by objects that run by themselves, we encounter little that challenges us to think in three dimensions. Our minds take on jobs, but our bodies are not employed. Physical work—with its wasted time, inefficiency, lazy detours—is different from efficient machines that don't do anything useless, but that also don't laugh or make jokes, that don't get embarrassed or embarrass us, or have ambition, an important part of any job.

Now that computers are able to read, write, and understand text-based data, consume large amounts of information, analyze and synthesize what's been learned, make it digestible, and predict outcomes, "knowledge workers" may develop a new humility. Physical workers in my practice never undervalue themselves, even if we fail to appreciate them and send them to the front lines, relatively undefended, during the outbreak of an infectious disease.

AN UNSURPRISING NUMBER OF ESSENTIAL workers got sick during COVID-19; some died. The next airborne pathogen will produce the same, maybe worse. But at least you may know better who these people are and how they think about their work.

# ACKNOWLEDGMENTS

My thousands of patients over the years came in looking for help and, along the way, helped me, sharing their stories, explaining what they did all day and how they felt about their hard work. Thank you to them. Carl Bromley at Melville House did much to improve the manuscript, and he made these pieces into a workable book. Thanks to Theresa Cameron and Michael Lindgren at Melville for special word care, and Dennis Johnson and Valerie Merians for their generous support. Tobias Stein, Alexander Stein, and Hester Kaplan listened to me talk about this project endlessly as I was writing it, and thankfully, they talked back. They are wise and loving. They all also like to hold a physical book in their hands, the best encouragement for writing one.

# SOURCES

## INTRODUCTION

*Centers for Disease Control.* From www.cdc.gov.

Chen YH, Glymour M, Riley A, et al. (2021) *Excess mortality associated with the COVID-19 pandemic among Californians 18–65 years of age, by occupational sector and occupation: March through November 2020.* PLoS ONE 16(6): e0252454. https://doi.org/10.1371/journal.pone.0252454

McCormack G, Avery C, Spitzer AKL, et al. (2020) *Economic vulnerability of households with essential workers. JAMA.* 324(4):388-390. From jamanetwork.com.

*State of Remote Work, 2019.* From owllabs.com.

Maestas N, Mullen KJ, Powell D, Wachter TV, Wenger JB. *Working Conditions in the United States. Results of the 2015 American working conditions survey.* From www.rand.org.

Lagorce T. (2023) "Plight of the 'Physical Worker': Worn-Out Bodies and Little Savings." *The New York Times.* June 21, 2023. From www.nytimes.com.

Sandel MJ. "Disdain for the Less Educated Is the Last Acceptable Prejudice." *The New York Times*, September 2, 2020. From www.nytimes.com.

## IDENTITY

Graeber D. (2018) *Bullshit Jobs: A Theory*. Simon & Schuster.

Plato. (1991) *The Republic of Plato*. Basic Books.

Bivens J, Engdahl L, Gould E, et. al., (2017) "How today's unions help working people." Economic Policy Institute. From www.epi.org.

## LOSSES

Pinckney D. (2022) "Our Lady of Deadpan." The *New York Review*. From www.nybooks.com.

Krueger AB. (2017) "Where Have All the Workers Gone? An Inquiry into the Decline of the U.S. Labor Market Participation Rate." *Brookings Papers*. From www.brookings.edu.

Venkataramani AS, Bair EF, O'Brien R, et al. (2020) "Association Between Automotive Assembly Plant Closures and Opioid Overdose Mortality in the United States: A Difference-in-Differences Analysis." *JAMA Internal Medicine* 180(2):254-262. doi:10.1001/jamainternmed.2019.5686. From jamanetwork.com.

Kurtzleben D. (2015) "Lots of Other Countries Mandate Paid Leave. Why Not the U.S.?" *National Public Radio*. From www.npr.org.

United States Interagency Council on Homelessness. (2024) Data and Trends. From www.usich.gov.

Desilver D. (2017) "Most Americans unaware that as U.S. manufacturing jobs have disappeared, output has grown." Pew Research Center. From www.pewresearch.org.

## CONNECTIONS

Andersen E. (2016) "Mike Rowe: Stop 'Cherry-Picking' One Form of Education." *National Review*. www.nationalreview.com.

Smith TW. (2007) "Job Satisfaction in the United States." NORC/ University of Chicago. From www.gbdioc.org.

Denning S. (2011) "Think Your Job Is Bad? Try One of These!" *Forbes*. www.forbes.com.

Oxfam. (2014) "From Paycheck to Pantry. Hunger in Working America." From www.feedingamerica.org.

U.S. Equal Opportunity Employment. (2024) Denying a leave request. From www.eeoc.gov.

## SURVIVAL

Terkel S. (1972) *Working*. New Press.

Stein MD. (2020) *Broke*. University of North Carolina Press.

Corley TC. (2016) *Change Your Habits, Change Your Life*. North Loop Books.

Bunn T, Bush A, Slavova S. (2014) "Drug overdose deaths by specific employment industry, occupation, and drug type." Journal of the Kentucky Medical Association 112:201–211.

Bureau of Labor Statistics. (2022) "National census of fatal occupational injuries." From www.bls.gov.

Bureau of Labor Statistics. (2022) "Employer-reported workplace injuries and illnesses." From www.bls.gov.

## STRUCTURE

Bureau of Labor Statistics. (2024) "Employer costs for employee compensation—March 2024." From www.bls.gov.

Bureau of Labor Statistics. (2006) "100 Years of U.S. Consumer Spending." From www.bls.gov.

## CODA

St-Esprit M. (2019) "The Stigma of Choosing Trade School over College." *The Atlantic*. From www.theatlantic.com.

National Center for Education Statistics. (2017) nces.ed.gov.

Erikson E. (1993) *Childhood and Society*. New York: W. W. Norton.